The Gen-Z Survival Guide to Neo-Fascism

© 2025 Rebel Healing Press. All rights reserved.
The Survival Guide to Neo-Fascism

No part of this publication may be reproduced, stored in a retrieval system, or transmitted in any form or by any means, electronic, mechanical, photocopying, recording, or otherwise, without the prior written permission of the publisher, except in the case of brief quotations embodied in critical articles or reviews.

Published by Rebel Healing Press
First Edition, 2025

I. Manifesto:
The Fool's Wake-Up Call

A wave of neo-fascism is moving through the United States, shaping its path through calculated deceit. The spell is subtle, it preys on struggle, hijacks rebellion, and uses psychological manipulation to divide people while pretending to empower them. Old hierarchies are coming back, rebuilt through tech systems and bureaucratic control. When those in power decide who can speak, what can be said, and when it can be heard, they're not protecting peace, they're enforcing obedience. Free speech is a birthright. When it gets rationed, that isn't the defense of democracy, it is authoritarian control.

II. What is Happening Now

- Freedom of speech and constitutional protections are increasingly conditional, often constrained when expression challenges political or corporate interests. Protest is reframed as extremism and dissent recast as a threat to national security.
- Mahmoud Khalil, a Palestinian-rights activist, and lawful U.S. resident who helped lead major campus protests demanding divestment from Israel, is now facing deportation. The administrative power has moved to revoke his green card without charging him with a crime, invoking a rarely used Cold War–era immigration clause meant for spies and national-security threats. That provision lets the Secretary of State deport anyone whose presence is deemed to have "potentially serious adverse foreign-policy consequences for the United States."
- Rumeysa Ozturk, a Turkish doctoral student was detained by ICE after co-authoring an op-ed in the student newspaper calling for the university to acknowledge the Palestinian genocide. The State Department revoked her visa, saying the U.S. "does not tolerate glorifying and supporting terrorists who kill Americans." After she was detained, ICE transferred her to a Processing Center, which is notorious for unsanitary conditions and harsh punitive measures.
- Across the country, students who speak out in support for Palestine or against genocide have faced blacklists, doxxing, detention, deportation, academic retaliation, and job threats.
- State-level anti-protest laws have redefined 'rioting,' granted legal immunity to drivers who hit protestors, and criminalized mass mobilization. This is not about national security, its suppression. The illusion of democracy is maintained only for the obedient and privileged. For everyone else, the crackdown is already here.

- Under the banner of "Making D.C. Safe and Beautiful," President Trump temporarily placed D.C. police operations under federal command, deploying over 1,400 National Guard troops, ICE agents, and Park Police across the capital. Hundreds were arrested, more than 70 homeless encampments cleared, and immigrant raids carried out, all in a city with crime already at a 30-year low. It was a show of force in the one city where he doesn't need a governor's consent, a warning of how far that power could spread. "Get out and vote, just this time," Trump told his supporters. "You won't have to do it anymore. Four more years, you know what, it'll be fixed, it'll be fine. You won't have to vote anymore, my beautiful Christians."

- Pentagon documents revealed that President Trump is pushing for a "Domestic Civil Disturbance Quick Reaction Force," 600 National Guard troops in Alabama and Arizona, ready to storm U.S. cities within an hour. The claim of security could be exploited, giving the presidency unchecked control to deploy troops against fundamental rights and freedoms, including the right to assembly and freedom of speech.

- In August 2025, more than 50 Texas Democrats fled the state to block a Republican redistricting plan that would cement one-party rule. Lawmakers hid in out-of-state locations while GOP leaders threatened to have them returned under escort, an openly authoritarian tactic.

- Leaked group chats from the Young Republican National Federation exposed open white-supremacist rhetoric: Hitler memes, racist slurs, and antisemitic jokes. The same ideology fuels a growing network of far-right clubs, militant fight groups spreading across the U.S. and Europe. Together they reveal how fascism hides behind patriotism and youth politics, rebranding itself as nationalism.

- In 2025, Trump signed an executive order designating Antifa as a domestic terrorist organization, even though it isn't a structured group under U.S. law. The move gave federal agencies broad authority to investigate and detain anyone accused of "affiliation," effectively allowing the state to treat political dissent as terrorism. Branding demonstrators, Anti-war activists, Pro-Palestine, and Anti-genocide protesters as Antifa to justify surveillance and arrests.

III. Targeting of Minority Groups

Early fascist regimes thrived by scapegoating already-marginalized groups: Jewish people, Romani and Polish people, disabled people, and political dissidents, to divide and conquer. Today's neo-fascists use the same playbook, but now include the target of immigrants, Muslims, trans people, and other vulnerable communities as "threats." The faces change, but the strategy stays the same: divide, dehumanize, and dominate. Authoritarians recruit through fear and prejudice, using these forces to build a cult-like following. Transforming private frustration into public rage, where ordinary people feel safe to unleash what they once suppressed, turning buried resentment into a weapon of mass control. When hostility becomes normalized, people feel free to act on impulses once kept in check. Compassion becomes naïve, and cruelty becomes emotional permission for their own self-contempt and unprocessed pain.

A defining feature of neo-fascism is its drive to restore a rigid, patriarchal social order rooted in conservative ideology. It relies on state power to enforce traditional gender roles, punish autonomy, and present the control of others' freedoms as "moral righteousness."

As seen in:

- The overturning of *Roe v. Wade* marked a turning point in the onset of U.S. neo-fascism, not just a rollback of rights, but a signal that bodily autonomy is conditional under religious-nationalist rule. It reflects the fascist impulse to sanctify patriarchal authority over women's anatomy in the name of moral purity. The stripping of reproductive rights often targets the most vulnerable, poor women, minorities, and those without healthcare access. Just as women were once viewed as property with no say in matters of life and death, today, a woman's life can now be sacrificed for the sake of church and state-imposed beliefs. Dozens of states rapidly enacted total or near-total abortion bans. Astonishingly, many without exceptions for medical, rape, or incest, blocking life-saving care, and reducing them to vessels of reproduction rather than living, breathing, free citizens.

- New bans and restrictions on transgender people in the military are part of a wider assault on LGBTQ+ rights. Protections for both gay and trans Americans have been rolled back through administrative changes and policy reversals, including the removal of sexual orientation and gender identity information from federal websites, cuts to inclusive healthcare and adoption policies, and escalating censorship of representation in schools and media.

- Mexican and Latin American immigrants are routinely demonized as criminals, rapists, or "invaders," a narrative designed to manufacture fear and justify state aggression. Even legal residents and non-criminal migrants face detention and deportation under policies that treat migration as a threat rather than a human reality. Families have been separated, parents imprisoned, and children held in detention centers under conditions that strip them of dignity and due process. As Umberto Eco warned in his point *"Fear of Difference,"* fascism always requires a scapegoat, an outsider to blame, dehumanize, and punish to unite the "pure" against the imagined threat found in immigrants and LGBTQ+.

IV. Fascist Coalitions and Alliances

- Evangelical leaders declared Trump "chosen by God," mobilizing a mass base to push for policies restricting bodily autonomy, LGBTQ+ rights, and public education. They also poured millions into his campaign.
- Billionaire political donors, including Sheldon and Miriam Adelson, poured over $90 million into Trump's campaign to push U.S. support for Israeli territorial expansion. This included the controversial relocation of the U.S. embassy to Jerusalem, a move that effectively legitimized Zionist occupation and apartheid.
- Tech oligarchs like Elon Musk, Trump's largest donor and owner of X, buys his way into the white house, leverages his platform to normalize far-right ideology, dismantle democratic norms, and amplify extremist narratives under the guise of 'free speech.'

These alliances function as pillars of modern American fascism because they use state power and tech to impose a narrow, religious, and nationalist ideology on the entire population. In return, Trump cut taxes for the rich, gutted public programs, and handed courts and diplomacy to those aligned with white Christian and Zionist nationalist interests. Trump wasn't campaigning on "America First" for the people. He was delivering for the billionaires and religious leaders who put him in office. Behind closed doors, he floated annexing Canada, endorsed permanent Israeli control over the Jordan River Valley, and proposed building a U.S.-backed luxury "riviera" in Gaza, over Palestinian land, and graves.

These policies reflect a deeper alignment with neo-fascist ideologies, where government control is wielded to enforce exclusion, suppress resistance, and maintain control over marginalized populations. It's part of a global far-right vision: settler-colonial powers seizing land, justifying violence with religion, nationalism, and profit in an authoritarian frenzy.

In the 2024 U.S. federal election cycle, billionaires contributed a record $2.6 billion, more than doubling their donations from four years prior, with the majority supporting Republican candidates and causes aligned with authoritarian and nationalist policies. This substantial financial backing has facilitated the implementation of policies that suppress opposition, erode democratic institutions, and promote ethno-nationalist ideologies, effectively intertwining private capital with state power to advance neo-fascist and technocratic objectives. Billionaire corporations essentially run our country, consolidating power and pushing a corporate agenda.

V. Neoliberal Alignment

I. Unlike historical fascism's approach of 'national socialism' and expanded state control, today's neofascist movement has evolved from neoliberal globalization's aftermath. The far right preaches small government but what it wants is selective control, while opposing state regulation of business it demands state regulation of people. That split—freedom for markets, control for citizens—is the core of modern authoritarian politics. Globalization concentrated economic power in corporations. Authoritarians wants this too but to add social power to the formula—deciding who belongs, who is punished, and who gets excluded. The same end goal continues through privatization, but now through churches, surveillance, and law enforcement to dominate identity and conduct. Globalization shifted production to poorer countries, where cheap labor and few regulations fueled record corporate profits. It wiped out local markets, weakened workers' rights everywhere, and left many countries trapped in debt or dependency. All while costing millions of American jobs and shrinking the middle class. Wealth concentrated at the top, while communities, both abroad and at home, bore the cost. Neofascism re-emerges as the political response to that dislocation, offering identity in place of security and using nationalism and tradition to create the illusion of a return to normalcy. The transfer of authority from citizens to markets and from the public to the private prioritizes economic interests over social welfare and concentrates power among elites, achieving through economic means what traditional fascism accomplished through direct state control, until profit itself becomes the language of power. Neoliberalism built the global hierarchy; fascism attempts to militarize it. When global markets rule, democracy becomes a borderless economy with no citizens, only consumers. Both systems are designed to transform democratic power into profitable submission. When wealth is the only means to power, the road from neoliberalism to neofascism is shorter than we dare admit.

II. Principles of Liberation

Our Birthrights

- **Freedom of Speech:** We the people defend our First Amendment right to speak, protest, and dissent, even when it challenges those in power.
- **Bodily Autonomy:** No system owns our bodies, identities, or reproductive choices.
- **Radical Democracy:** We believe in freedom of thought, and decision-making by the people, not by billionaires, media, courts, or algorithms.
- **Economic Liberation:** Survival should not depend on exploitation. We reject crony capitalism's cycles of poverty, debt, and wage slavery to serve a few.

- **Anti-Authoritarianism:** No fascists, no boss, no state, no party will decide our future and personal or health rights for us.
- **Ecological Stewardship:** We protect the Earth not as property, but as our mother, as our beloved home and an interdependent ecosystem worthy of respect.
- **Digital Autonomy:** We demand control over our data, our platforms, and our digital lives, not surveillance by tech giants, corporations, or states.
- **Community over Corporations:** We value mutual aid, solidarity, regenerative economies, and local power over monopolies and markets.
- **Justice Over Order:** We reject "law and order" when it serves oppression and privatizers. True justice rehabilitates, heals, and transforms.
- **Liberation for All:** No one is free until everyone is free, equality and humanity across race, gender, class, ability, borders, and beyond.

VIII. What We The People Reject

We reject the foundations of neo-fascism and the empires it protects.

- We reject a plutocratic oligarchy, an economic system that has been weaponized to profit from exploitation, feeds inequality, and reduces human life to labor and consumption.
- We reject patriarchal systems, the global system of colonization, prejudice hierarchy, cultural genocide, and greed that perpetuate oppression and harm.
- We reject corporate power, unelected billionaires, tech monopolies, and lobbyists who write our laws and further oppress our future generations.
- We reject extremism and hatred in every form, including antisemitism, Islamophobia, racism, and xenophobia.
- We reject religious nationalism, the use of faith to justify oppression, take away freedom, deny science, and legislate morality.
- We reject the police state, surveillance, militarized policing, and the criminalization of protest and homelessness.
- We reject imperialism, military occupation, the bombing of civilians, the genocide of Palestinians, and the economic domination of people across the globe.
- We reject fundamentalism, the ideology that treats women, queer, and trans people as threats to tradition.
- We reject censorship disguised as safety, where solidarity is criminalized and free speech is punished when it challenges the state.
- We reject AI-driven control, where tech is used to automate surveillance, manipulate opinion, suppress intellect, and crush resistance.

- We reject climate and planet destruction for profit, and the fossil fuel billionaires burning the planet for short-term gain.

IX. What We The People Demand

- **Decolonize Everything:** Culture back. Power back. Return land where possible, Honor and restore Indigenous sovereignty. Agreements need to be honored, and reparations served.
- **People Over Profit:** Food, water, housing, education, and healthcare must be protected as basic rights, publicly funded, community-driven, and free from corporate and privatized control. We do not consent to universities, healthcare systems, and other institutions to profit from exploitation and war.
- **Tech Liberation:** End surveillance capitalism. Build decentralized, open-source platforms that empower people, not corporations. Ban algorithmic policing and biometric control that violate privacy and deepen oppression. We must reclaim control of the technologies that shape our lives and reject systems that surveil and profit off us.
- **No Profit in Punishment:** The Black community has long been targeted by policing and punishment systems rooted in racism and designed to preserve racial and economic hierarchy. Ban private prisons. Reform for-profit policing and prohibit racial profiling. Redirect resources into Black communities through healthcare access, community programs, and restorative justice.
- **Universal Bodily Autonomy:** Every adult has the right to transition, to abort, to love, free from surveillance, criminal charges, or state interference. Your body is yours. The state has no place in your decisions. We will not accept strict restrictions on autonomy under any guise.
- **Climate Reparations Now:** Hold the worst polluters accountable, forcing those who profited from planetary destruction to pay for repair and restoration. Climate justice means redistributing the stolen wealth of the carbon economy back into frontline communities, ocean and ecosystem restoration, and regenerative infrastructure. To truly confront this crisis, we must shift our priorities, ensuring that the planet's oceans, forests, and ecosystems are restored, respected, and protected, and that the wealth extracted from their exploitation is reinvested in sustainable, regenerative practices.
- **Public Education for the People**: No to charter school scams. No to corporate curriculum. Fully fund public schools, raise teacher wages, and protect classrooms from political censorship. Education must serve liberation, not obedience, teaching real history, critical thinking, and the tools to resist oppression.
- **End Mass Deportations and Immigration Bans.** No human is illegal. We must prioritize global solidarity and human dignity over nationalist fear, fostering

systems that offer refuge, opportunity, and fairness and humanity to all, while honoring the needs and capacities of the communities and ecosystems that sustain us.

- **Democratize the Economy:** End corporate socialism, no more bailouts, state-backed favoritism that funnels public money upward through contracts, subsidies, tax incentives, deregulation, and privatization deals. Break up monopolies, cancel the public's debt, and implement progressive taxation for the ultra-wealthy. Redirect public resources from corporate and private handouts toward regenerative solutions that prioritize the health of people and the planet over profit.

X. Power Is With the People They Fear Most

We stand with:

- Youth and freedom fighters rising up for equality
- The workers organizing
- The migrants fighting unjust deportation and detention
- The Indigenous protectors of land, nature, and truth
- The trans and queer people refusing erasure
- The communities targeted for their race, gender, faith, or identity
- The parents, teachers, and activists resisting censorship
- The sick, disabled, and suffering demanding access
- The whistleblowers, journalists, and truth-tellers
- The artists, hackers, healers, and rebels
- Everyone who's been told to sit down, shut up, or stay in their place in the name of oppression and refuses

We're not here to keep playing along with systems built on fear, hate, poverty, and destruction. We're the generation breaking the cycle — we're not handing down another round of war and greed. Direct action isn't complicated: stop being passive while people and the planet take the hit. Pull your support from companies causing harm. Protect anyone the state targets. Build community structures that actually care for people. This is how we choose justice and honesty every day. The future belongs to the ones who refuse exploitation, repair what was broken, and uplift the voices people in power try to silence.

I. The Tower: When False Reality Crumbles. Know Thy System

To understand this broader socially engineered system, you have to understand how it sees you. Not as a human being. Not as a citizen, but as a product, consumer, liability, and just another number in a profit formula.

The ruling class of corporations, billionaires, and the politicians they own do not build systems to serve the people. They build systems to tolerate and manage the population and maximize extraction. They operate from one foundational belief: The masses are dumb, complacent, and easily manipulated.

Every industry from healthcare to agriculture, from media to energy operates on the assumption that your survival is secondary to their quarterly growth.

- Healthcare creates a business model from disease, chronic illness, vaccines, and pills, not holistically from the root cause.
- Industrial food systems sell us toxic, processed, chemically enriched products while stripping us of the right to grow real food. They patent seeds, hoard land, and pass laws that make self-sufficiency illegal, unsustainable, or out of reach.
- Technology companies manufacture consent for surveillance capitalism, collecting your data, tracking your behavior, and selling it to advertisers and government agencies through engineered addiction.
- Large corporations and their lobbyists do more than pollute. Behind the veil of public relations and marketing, they influence legislation, control elections, suppress wages, exploit global labor, dodge taxes, and destabilize entire economies. They fund think tanks to shape public opinion, lobby lawmakers to kill regulations, and outsource harm to countries with fewer protections. They control food systems, energy grids, military, medical research, digital infrastructure, and public education. They operate with zero public accountability, but enormous political power. And they rely on your compliance, your consumption, and your silence to keep the system running.

You are kept overworked and distracted not by accident, but by design. A sick, anxious, isolated population is easier to sell to, control, and pacify. The more disconnected you are from your health, your community, and nature, the more dependent you become on the very systems causing the crisis.

And while we are taught to argue over two-party politics, identity, and headlines, those in power are poisoning the planet beyond repair, destroying oceans, clear-cutting forests, destabilizing the climate, and collapsing biodiversity. Why? Because the profit window is closing. And their strategy is to extract everything they can before it's over.

Meanwhile, we're conditioned to accept atrocities, genocide, and barbarism as normal. This is a manufactured crisis of consciousness; an effort to disconnect us from reality, dulls our instinct, and weakens our ability to recognize truth or solidarity. We are taught not to question it, apathy vs empathy, and to adapt to the absurdity. Oppressors subliminally encourage us to treat ourselves and others as expendable and to praise their exploitation progress under some gaslighting hypnosis campaign. Step back and see the patterns. And realize that the system is not broken, it is perfectly engineered to keep us obedient, divided, and distracted, while it profits from every form of decay.

II. The Rise of Neo-Fascism

Neoliberalism, with its ruthless emphasis on free markets, deregulation, and privatization, has systematically turned healthcare, education, and the environment into commodities, left social safety nets in ruins. Under the corporate seizure, inequality implodes and communities fracture; people are left detached, desperate, and disposable in a system that measures every human need by its profit margin.

In that manufactured vacuum, fascist leaning ideologies take root as emotional refuge, offering belonging in exchange for obedience. With fewer protections and amplified fear, millions turn to authoritarian movements that promise simple solutions to complex pain, a return to nostalgia, where surveillance, nationalism, religious law, militarized streets, and algorithmic control replace democratic life, paving the way for modern fascism to seize power. In the 1990s, the Italian writer and philosopher Umberto Eco, who lived through Mussolini's regime, warned that fascism was not a relic but a recurring pattern. In his essay "Ur-Fascism," he highlighted the red flags. Three of the most current visible points we illustrate in this text are the *cult of tradition*, the *rejection of modernism*, and *obsession with a plot*, all re-emerging through a global wave of anti-intellectualism. It's the cult of ritual and group-think over reasoning. Anti-intellectualism has become a side effect of a political strategy: the deliberate replacement of critical thinking with spectacle. When president Donald Trump releases an AI video depicting himself defecating on protesters, and his supporters cheer at crude lines that mock truth, it isn't humor, it's indoctrination of infantilism and anti-reason for the sake of tribalism. It says more about our collective shadow than it does about the leader.

Co-opting Social Causes: The Facade of 'Woke Capitalism'

In an attempt to maintain relevance and consumer loyalty, many corporations have adopted the language of social justice. While these companies outwardly support progressive causes, their core operations frequently contradict the very values they publicly endorse. For instance, a corporation might champion diversity and be eco-conscious in its greenwashing marketing campaigns while simultaneously engaging in exploitative labor practices or contributing to environmental degradation. This superficial alignment with social causes serves more as a branding strategy than a genuine commitment to systemic change, effectively commodifying activism and diluting the potency of grassroots movements as phony, irrelevant, or extremist.

The Intersection of Neoliberalism and Neo-Fascism

The alliance between neoliberal economic policies and emerging neo-fascist ideologies is not coincidental. Neoliberalism's focus on individualism and market supremacy erodes collective social values by prioritizing profit over people. As inequality worsens and unrest grows, neo-fascist groups exploit the chaos, blaming marginalized communities and lack of tradition, pushing authoritarian "solutions" that promise order but only shift the form of oppression administered.

Understanding the symbiotic cycle where neoliberal policies exacerbate societal issues, and neo-fascist ideologies capitalize on the resulting unrest is key to seeing how these policies fuel social decay, and how that decay opens the door to authoritarian rule. To confront one is to confront both. If we want to defend democracy, we must address the root causes: manufactured fear and scarcity, engineered trauma and inequality, systemic disempowerment, and the corporate capture and two-party cartel that sustains them to accumulate wealth and power.

So, What's the Antidote to Neo-Fascism?

We don't beat authoritarianism and fascism by doubling down on the same system that made it possible. Most folks want the same things: safety, dignity, equality, housing, autonomy, healthcare, truth. The problem isn't the people we may not identify with; it's the program we have all been sold.

The antidote to neofascism isn't a return to a "safer" neoliberal "normalcy." It's taking back control of the essentials that shape our lives and pulling them out of corporate hands. Rebuilding local economies means supporting worker-owned cooperatives instead of exploitative employers, investing in community land trusts that protect homes from speculation, and redirecting public funds toward small farmers and local producers instead of agribusiness monopolies. It means creating local energy grids powered by renewables, municipal broadband that guarantees access to truth over propaganda, and local banks that finance people, not profit. Real resistance looks like organized labor, mutual aid networks, and public institutions accountable to the communities they serve, not to shareholders or donors. Fascism feeds on disempowerment; the cure must be in the organized disruption and collective rebuilding, taking back power through how we live, work, and consume. Start locally.

III. Whether neoliberalism's polite empire or neofascism's brute-force nationalism, both rely on the same mechanisms:

- Manufactured consent, Psychological warfare, Intellectual distortion, Algorithmic censorship, Fear-based obedience, Engineered scarcity.
- Co-opts social justice or conservative language to sell you the same oppression with a rainbow logo or religious symbol.
- Supports endless war, corporate bailouts, and mass surveillance, only with better PR. Neoliberalism doesn't fight fascism, it only gentrifies it.

When neoliberalism's shiny lies no longer pacify the masses, the gloves come off. Enter neo-fascism, same empire, less subtle, less dignified.

- Blame minorities, activists, immigrants, and progressives as extremists or criminals.
- Justify police and protest brutality and censorship as "necessary protection."
- Taking away our freedom of speech, a Constitutional guarantee regardless of citizenship, marks the first fatal step toward authoritarianism, now that suppression is carried out by corporations shielded by law.
- Uses manufactured chaos as a pretext for more surveillance, more militarization, and more control.
- Deploys social media as a psychological warfare zone to keep us scared, numb, and divided.
- Divide, Distract, Destroy mantra reflected across social media troll farms and patriotic propaganda

This is the engine of cognitive dissonance:

- Pick a scapegoat then flood the media with outrage. Twist truth into partisan identity and weaponize our trauma into tribalism.

- All the while, the real villains sit comfortably in public office, funded by the very billionaires running your social media feed and news, your pharmacy, your food supply, and your healthcare "choices."

We are conditioned into false ideologies, the illusions of left and right that create separation, complacency, and helplessness. The debate becomes an endless trap by design.

IV. How Fascism Rose Before. We've Seen this Movie Before.

Italy (Mussolini): Fascism = Corporatism

- "Fascism should more properly be called corporatism, since it is the merger of state and corporate power."
- He outlawed unions, used state terror to silence dissidents, and aligned business elites with state authority. Economic production was centralized in the hands of a few, and war was a tool to "reignite the nation."

Spain (Franco): Religion + Fascism = Thought Control

- Franco fused nationalism with Catholicism, banning regional languages, jailing intellectuals, and erasing queer and leftist identities.
- It was ideological warfare. If you weren't on board, you disappeared into prisons, mass graves, or forced labor.

Germany (Hitler): Total Control through Economic Collapse

- *Backdrop*: Post-WWI Germany was broke, humiliated, and politically fractured. The Weimar Republic was drowning in debt. Hyperinflation was so bad people used money as wallpaper.
- Hitler rode in on a wave of nationalist rage and desperation. His strategy? Blame the Jewish people and marginalized, build a cult of personality, rewrite the truth with mass propaganda and misinformation, and promise restored "order."
- Fascism has always relied on corporate power. In Nazi Germany, companies like Volkswagen, BMW, IG Farben, and Siemens used forced labor from concentration camps and profited heavily from arms manufacturing and war. The regime handed the economy to loyal industrialists. Sound Familiar?

Today, the formula created by neoliberalism in the 1980s has not changed, just the sides. The current administration and its donors use the Trump presidency to deregulate industries, cut corporate taxes, and build alliances with fossil fuel, weapons, and tech billionaires. He handed federal contracts to companies like Palantir, Amazon, and private prison corporations while attacking labor, immigrants, and the press. Trump's tariffs and "America First" are a corporate takeover disguised as patriotism. By making imports unaffordable, they systematically destroy small businesses that can't absorb the costs, clearing the market for mega-corporations that can. Meanwhile, these same corporations pass every tariff cost not to foreign exporters, but to the American consumers and importers, profiting from both the inflation they create and the competition they eliminate. The endgame was always consolidation: fewer competitors, higher prices, captive consumers, and grateful corporations funneling campaign cash back to the politicians who handed them monopoly power.

Elon Musk plays the same game: selling "free speech" while manipulating algorithms, selectively enforcing rules, making deals with law enforcement, and building surveillance tech and AI under the guise of innovation. Musk doesn't just want government contracts; he wants to BE the government. Through Starlink, he controls global internet access. Through Neuralink, he's positioning to control human consciousness itself. Through SpaceX, he's building the infrastructure for off-world escape routes for the ultra-wealthy when resources run dry. Musk positions himself as a visionary outsider while embedding himself in state contracts, defense projects, and social engineering schemes that further the merger of tech and authoritarian power. The corporate-state apparatus that tracks, predicts, and ultimately governs human behavior, with Musk as the unelected emperor of digital existence.

Both have cultivated dangerous cults of personality, positioning themselves as saviors while demanding blind loyalty. They've co-opted people's legitimate frustrations, the democratic party's betrayal, convincing them that democracy itself is broken and only these strongmen can fix it. In reality, their actions serve to centralize power, exploit greater resources, and stifle resistance. This is what neofascism looks like today: a mostly unelected elite and big tech consolidating power, silencing opposition, restoring the rule of tradition, church and state, and gradually reshaping society for profit and more strict control until before you know it freedom is something you have to risk your life to remember, and obedience becomes the price of survival.

Unaccountable large corporations have become the primary engine of modern authoritarianism and neofascism. When corporations are shielded from consequences, and writes the laws that regulate them, and permitted to control our resources, information, and labor, democratic power dies. The state no longer represents the people, it protects profit. In this system, repression will not directly announce itself as fascism, because it is quietly enforced through contracts, data, debt, privatization, and economic manipulation. This is why the way out is ending corporate and concentrated private power over public life.

1930s Fascism	2020s Neo-Fascism
Militarized nationalism	"America First," anti-immigrant & queer policies, ICE raids
Corporate-state fusion	Amazon + DHS, Palantir + ICE, Big Pharma and Tech lobbying
State propaganda	"Neutral" social platforms, woke right campaign, influencer-led psyops
Book burning	**Algorithmic** censorship, info floods, shadow banning
Secret police	Mass surveillance, technocratic enforcement, predictive policing, data brokers
Eugenics rhetoric	AI bias and social scores, reproductive control, biometric border tech
Political prisons	Cash bail, private prisons, ICE detention, RICO charges on protestors
Scapegoating "the other"	Anti-trans legislation, xenophobic refugee policies, anti-Black policing, and incarceration

Reclaiming Truth : Neofascism feeds on lies, fear, prejudice, and collectivism. Neoliberalism feeds on engineered trauma, moral branding, exploiting both equality and individualism. This means unlearning what we were taught in school, in the media, in history books. It means learning from each other, history, from the land, and the people silenced. The antidote then is unify. Unlearning the myth of separation and division to see inherit truth. We unite through collective sense-making, find common ground, and recognize each system's arm as a source of harm. We stop feeding it, detach from it, and build a unified movement with real solutions that don't depend on the old system.

I. THE DEVIL:
The Man, The Myth, The Cult, The Oppressors

When the state-media-corporate complex co-opts, distorts, and exploits real struggles: bodily autonomy, queer rights, racial justice, are stripped of context, exaggerated, and reframed as threats to "traditional values." This is how the system preserves itself: by turning modernism into threat. By turning human rights into partisan targets, the ruling class divides the public and discredits the movements demanding real change.

- Abortion becomes a wedge issue, not a freedom, healthcare, or lifesaving right but a demographic control mechanism
- LGBTQ+ people become political props instead of human beings under attack.
- Anti-racism is reduced to "wokeness."
- Feminism becomes "radical leftism."
- Environmentalism becomes "eco-terrorism."

Once these issues are politicized and polarized, the system wins. The right attacks them. The left is trapped defending slogans. And the actual people or entities involved are forgotten in between both parties branding. This is identity politics as a device of state control, not to empower anyone, but to fracture solidarity and keep the public fighting over symbols and labels instead of truth and justice.

Genuine climate concerns are being co-opted. Instead of addressing the actual causes like fossil fuel extraction, industrial pollution, factory farming, land theft, corporate agriculture, governments, and corporations are using climate fears to justify new forms of control:

- Militarized borders are being expanded, not just to block climate refugees but to secure wealth and resources in 'developed' nations while leaving vulnerable populations to suffer from environmental collapse.
- Disaster capitalism thrives, where corporations capitalize on climate catastrophes to profit from rebuilding efforts, often through privatized solutions that make the rich richer and leave the poor vulnerable to the next disaster.
- Greenwashing is rampant, companies market themselves as environmentally conscious while continuing to extract resources, harm ecosystems, and rely on fossil fuel infrastructure, all while making a profit from vague "eco-friendly" products that don't change the fundamental issues at play.

- Resource privatization becomes a new tool for control, with the elites purchasing access to water, land, and other essential resources, while the rest of the population struggles with scarcity and inflation driven by these private monopolies.
- Eco-fascism: the use of environmental collapse to expand authoritarian power. Climate crisis becomes a pretext for control: privatization, normalizing apathy, and deciding who is disposable.

II.   Techno-Fascism

Techno-fascism, where technocracy fuses with authoritarianism, is the integration of corporate technology infrastructure with institutional power to monitor, influence, and control the public. It is not futurism, it's already here. The merger of tech monopolies with authoritarian politics has replaced traditional state functions with unaccountable private systems. Surveillance is no longer the role of the state alone. Under the guise of convenience and security, tech companies collect mass data, predict behavior, and shape public opinion. Governments now contract out control to these firms, who hold more intimate data than any intelligence agency ever could. The push to purchase TikTok isn't about privacy, it's about being threatened by platforms they don't fully control and keeping digital dominance in the hands of the U.S.-based surveillance empires.

Peter Thiel, co-founder of Palantir, a company built from early CIA funding, helped create one of the most powerful surveillance and data-analysis platforms in the world. Palantir supplies predictive policing and population-tracking technology to military and intelligence agencies, law enforcement, and immigration enforcement, including ICE. Its tools have been used to profile immigrants, monitor communities, and criminalize dissent with little transparency or public accountability. At the same time, Thiel has used his wealth to influence elections and support authoritarian-leaning movements, fusing surveillance infrastructure with political power in a way that mirrors classic elements of technofascism.

Amazon provides the cloud infrastructure for the CIA, DHS, and police departments across the country. It supplies facial recognition tools to law enforcement and holds contracts with ICE and Border Protection. At the same time, it breaks unions, surveils its workers, and punishes those who organize. Jeff Bezos profits from war logistics, surveillance infrastructure, deportation, and labor exploitation.

Mark Zuckerberg runs the largest behavioral influence platform in the world, filters organizing efforts, suppresses resistance, and monetizes polarization and surveillance. Meta (Facebook/Instagram) actively censors political and civil rights speech, rescue work, determines what information is visible to the public, and partners with the state to regulate online narratives. It allows state-sanctioned disinformation while silencing activists and resistance.

Elon Musk controls key infrastructure, satellites (Starlink), Tesla, and X. His military contracts and control over internet access in conflict zones place him in direct alignment with state and military interests. He led Trump's Department of Government Efficiency (DOGE), and gained access to sensitive systems, including the public's Treasury and IRS data. While he publicly mocks others for relying on government funding, Musk's empire is built on billions in federal contracts and subsidies. His consolidation of public and private power raises serious concerns about surveillance, a warning sign of technofascist consolidation.

Gen Z was born into the digital world. You learned the internet the way earlier generations learned language, which means the tools of control are woven into the same spaces where you socialize, organize, flirt, learn, escape, and cope. Instead of censorship through force, you get censorship through invisibility: posts pushed down, stories buried, voices throttled by "community guidelines" that never apply equally. Instead of propaganda plastered across billboards, you get tailored fear, micro-targeted outrage, and viral narratives designed to pull you toward one identity and away from another. Technofascism works best on people who can't tell the difference between what they're choosing and what they're being nudged toward. Gen Z's power is knowing the difference. The resistance is about refusing to let the algorithm decide who you are, what you believe, and who you stand with. It's about noticing the manipulation and choosing connection, intelligibility, and community anyway.

III.   Neo-Fascist and Authoritarian Movements

Identity and labeling are used as propaganda tools to divide the public and redirect rage. In states like Florida and Texas, politicians restricting basic education about slavery, civil rights, and systemic racism by falsely branding it "critical race theory." At the same time, they passed anti-trans laws and book bans to inflame culture war panic. These tactics serve a purpose: to manufacture outrage, pit communities against each other. The culture war is not about keeping tradition, it is to prevent solidarity, suppress resistance and individuality, consciousness, and create a culture and religious war as a smokescreen for authoritarian rule. This manipulation of ideology is one of the greatest drivers of intellectual regression. Where critical thought gives way to tribal loyalty, and the act of thinking for yourself is decimated.

In 2023, more than 500 anti-LGBTQ+ bills were introduced across the U.S., many written or backed by far-right networks and Christian nationalist groups. These laws criminalize care, erase identities, and cultivate fear. This isn't a matter of left or right—both parties serve the same alliance of religious zealotry and corporate power—but part of a broader movement to control bodies, beliefs, and public life. Authoritarian regimes have always policed gender and sexuality to re-enforce conformity and punish dissent. And Neoliberals have used it to buy votes and push hidden agendas that keep people further oppressed and divided.

LGBTQ+ people are targeted by neo-fascist movements because they reject the roles society tries to force on them. Fascist systems rely on control through tradition and uniformity, with clear rules about who you're allowed to be, how you're supposed to live, and who holds power, often reinforcing dangerous social hierarchies. Queer and trans people break those rules just by existing. They show that identity, gender, and freedom don't have to follow state-approved norms or constructs. This level of freedom and consciousness scares authoritarians. So, they attack it, through laws, media, and moral panic to push everyone back into rigid categories they can control. These attacks are backed by religious extremists and billionaire donors who fund the politicians and presidencies pushing these laws. Their goal is obedience, not safety, and they use moral panic to expand state power and erase anyone who doesn't fit into their carefully checked boxes of conformity.

Weaponized Wokeness

"Wokeness" began as a leftist grassroots call for awareness and action around injustice and prejudice, a powerful and positive force for social justice movements.

Neoliberal leaders didn't adopt leftist woke language to create real change though, they used it to advance their own agendas. By promoting highly visible, often symbolic policies around race, gender, and climate, they created political flashpoints that were easily manipulated for their own greed and votes. These moves appeared deceptive, deepened division, confused the public, and shifted attention away from deeper systemic issues. Climate change was used to funnel billions to private contractors. Trans people's rights were co-opted by politicians on both sides as political bait to stir fear, manipulate the public, exploit children, and split voters. The problem isn't the legitimacy of the causes themselves, but how politicians and media misuse them for power, turning real human struggles into tools of propaganda at the expense of the very communities that need protection.

The "woke" right (a term popularized by Jimmy Dore) co-opted the original term to position progressive social awareness as a threat to traditional values, individual liberties, and national identity. By labeling any discussion of systemic problems as "woke ideology," they can ban books, defund schools, and strip rights while claiming they're protecting freedom from radicalization. The strategy is both brilliant and absurd in its simplicity: make awareness of injustice seem more threatening than the injustice itself. The irony is that they've adopted the very language of resistance they mock, crying censorship and oppression while pushing laws that oppress and surveil. What remains is high-stage paranoia. As Eco noted the phenomena in "the Obsession with a Plot, and the Enemy Both Strong and Weak," a movement that is obsessed with race, gender, social conflict, and conspiracies, like addictive clickbait, convinced that so-called 'white and traditional America' is under siege. Subconsciously, recreating a new version of extremism they originally feared. Now, the term 'wokism' is overused and misused to divide the public. Real issues demanding resolution: like racism, queer rights, and systemic justice, become collateral damage in the crossfire of a manufactured culture war. These vital struggles are dismissed as trivial distractions or threats. The marginalized communities who originally sought healing and inclusion now find themselves scapegoated for the very divisions their activism aimed to overcome.

Women's Rights

Neofascist movements target women's autonomy because control over the body is essential to authoritarian rule, demographic control, and increased dependency on the system that keeps it running. After Roe v. Wade was overturned, states rushed to criminalize abortion, even in cases of rape, medical emergencies, or non-viable pregnancies. A 10-year-old rape victim in Ohio had to flee the state for care. In Texas, a doctor was arrested for performing a lifesaving abortion. In multiple states, pregnant women have died from sepsis and other medical complications because the law prevented them from receiving care. This is happening every day in a country that prides itself on being one of the wealthiest and most advanced democracies on Earth. Forced birth keeps people in cycles of poverty, dependence, and exhaustion. It strengthens patriarchal control, increases economic desperation, and reduces people's ability to organize or resist. Behind these policies are religious extremists and political networks using morality as cover to enforce submission and expand state control. When you control reproduction, you control the future. Babies are treated as future labor, trapped in cycles engineered by artificial scarcity. The proven ways to prevent unwanted pregnancies are not bans, but pathways to economic opportunity, education, healthcare, the very things these regimes defund because lowering birth rates is not aligned with their agenda. Empowering women through access to contraception, sex education, and reproductive healthcare leads to fewer abortions and stronger families. Taking away women's rights doesn't protect life. It perpetuates a cycle of poverty and intergenerational trauma that sustains the system.

I. The Moon
(The Mass Hypnosis)

We're not just misinformed; we're being mass manipulated. Gaslighting is used at scale through media and tech platforms to create cognitive dissonance, erode perception, and fracture reality in an echo chamber of premeditated homicide on our sanity. We're told two things at once. We're told nothing is true. Then we're told to pick a side and call it the only way.

This confusion is by design. It keeps the public unstable, divided, and reactive. Left and right-wing political machines fund influencers, media outlets, and content troll farms to push conflicting narratives that fuel outrage, not solutions. The result is structured chaos where we stop thinking for ourselves. We no longer work on solutions but engage in online info wars.

Every hour the narrative shifts. Every crisis is framed as partisan.

This creates cognitive dissonance, a mental overload where nothing feels fully true, so people retreat into whatever version of reality feels safest and familiar.

That's how echo chambers form. Social media algorithms, designed for engagement, feed us more of what speaks to our unprocessed trauma, that little child inside that is still angry and unheard. What we end up with are people operating from their wounded inner child, lashing out in public forums, in the white house, and making decisions that shape the world through our collective trauma. Corporate and partisan media do the same. We stop thinking critically and start reacting emotionally. Collective sense-making collapses into collective triggering. A society trauma-bonding instead of reasoning, mistaking what mirrors our denied shadow parts as truth. We're no longer shaping culture through ideas, but through wounds that never heal, letting our pain set the terms of every conversation.

Meanwhile, influencers across the political spectrum are paid to reinforce these divisions. They're backed by think tanks, campaign or PAC money, and algorithmic promotion delivering scripted outrage disguised as decentralized media. They're doing PR for billionaires and political operatives or running clickbait schemes to pad their pockets by exploiting a cause to push a party line.

And who owns the mass media? A handful of billionaire's corporations and tech monopolies. They control the headlines, the platforms, and the language. The result is a public in utter chaos, too divided and disoriented to organize, question power, or make sense of what's actually happening. Just stick with the popular left/right narrative and it will all be ok, right?

This is not just misinformation wars. It's a coordinated, profit-driven attack on our consciousness. The best thing one can do is disconnect and take real life action.

II. Algorithmic Radicalization and AI Psyops

Algorithms aren't neutral. They're engineered to maximize engagement because attention is profitable. Rage, fear, spectacle, and tribal loyalty drive more clicks than truth, compassion, or context. The result is a machine that rewards extremism, sensationalism, polarizes communities, and slowly erodes the public's ability to think critically.

Extremist groups, state actors, political machines, and corporations exploit this dynamic. Algorithms then radicalize and confuse users by pushing the ever-popular distortion of the truth. If hate content keeps people watching, it wins the algorithm war. If chaos drives traffic, it's boosted.

Now AI accelerates this even further. Deepfakes, synthetic audio, AI-generated misinformation, and psyops bots make it nearly impossible to know what's real. Fake accounts push extremist content under the radar, stoke division, or mimic grassroots movements to confuse and destabilize. When political leaders on both sides use AI-generated propaganda to mock or attack others, it normalizes cruelty and turns cyberbullying into entertainment. These are not the role models we want for children.

Clickbait is only the surface. The real aim is to manufacture consent by keeping the public in a state of chaos and confusion, where manipulation becomes effortless They begin to dissociate until someone makes them feel safe again. Trump said it best, "Maybe we like a dictator." When truth becomes uncertain, trust collapses, and in that void, fascists, demagogues, and billionaires step in to offer "clarity" through authority to the fragile psyche of the already unstable human user.

Governments and private intelligence firms use AI psyops to target protestors, discredit movements, and control public narrative. Platforms that claim to be "neutral" profit from the conflict and sell the data that feeds it. This is how modern propaganda works: it doesn't convince you of one lie. It shows you a thousand versions of the truth until you give up trying to tell the difference and accept the general narrative or the one that suits our own traumatized bias.

III. Shadow Government

Presidents change. The agenda and those ultimately in control don't.

What we call democracy is mostly theater. The real decisions, on war, civil rights, surveillance, trade, censorship, labor, and resources, are made by unelected power structures: intelligence agencies, defense contractors, corporate lobbies, and billionaire-controlled think tanks. This is the shadow government, not a conspiracy, but a network of influence that operates without public oversight.

These institutions shape politics. Intelligence agencies have historically funded and manipulated media narratives. Defense contractors and think tanks heavily influence foreign policy through lobbying, campaign donations, and revolving-door relationships. Private equity firms buy hospitals, prisons, schools, and housing, then lobby against regulation to protect profits. Billionaires bankroll politicians across party lines to ensure that, no matter who wins, their interests are protected. They have control over infrastructure, information, and capital. From Palantir to BlackRock to the Federal Reserve, these entities govern without ever being seen, through money, policy, and control of narrative.

They use national security as a shield and identity politics as cover. They exploit crises to expand surveillance. The public is left voting in a system where the outcome changes little, and the illusion of choice masks structural control. There is no deep state. It's the *actual state* that no one elected, but everyone is forced to quietly obey and live under.

This isn't new. From 1956 to 1971, the FBI ran COINTELPRO, a covert program to infiltrate, discredit, and destroy social movements. They targeted the Black Power Movement, anti-war organizers, Native resistance, feminist groups, and anyone challenging U.S. imperialism. They used informants, forged documents, and media manipulation to fracture movements and incite internal conflict. Martin Luther King Jr. was surveilled, harassed, and sent anonymous letters encouraging him to kill himself. The state department are masters in psychological warfare.

And while the FBI targeted movements, the CIA targeted perception. Through Operation Mockingbird, the agency secretly recruited journalists and infiltrated major U.S. media outlets to spread propaganda, control foreign policy narratives, and suppress stories that challenged U.S. interests. The public thought they were reading journalism, but they were reading state propaganda. This is how the infrastructure became privatized and still continues today. We can all learn something from the propaganda machine; conscious propaganda has the power to shift things and undo their technocratic witchcraft.

IV. Propaganda and Manufactured Consent: The Bernays Blueprint

Edward Bernays, nephew of Sigmund Freud, didn't just invent public relations. He built the playbook for how governments and corporations shape belief. His core idea: people don't make rational decisions, they respond to emotion, identity, sensationalism, and spectacle. So, if you want control, you don't need truth, you only need a great storyteller who invokes emotion. In today's political climate, that translates to someone who can summon people's unprocessed rage or shame and dress it up as righteousness.

He taught governments how to sell war, and corporations how to sell cigarettes as feminist rebellion. The elites took his masterclass in how to control public opinion by bypassing logic and appealing to fear, sex, trends, and belonging. He called it "engineering consent."

That same blueprint runs everything now, from corporate media to social platforms to influencer culture. Manufactured consent today is delivered in press conferences, by influencers, talking heads, and podcasters who exploit partial truths, conspiracies, and outrage as entertainment. They present themselves as anti-establishment while reinforcing the very systems they claim to oppose. Sensationalized half-truths are more dangerous than lies because they feel familiar and lead to widespread misinformation collectives. They borrow the tone of truth while hollowing it out from within. These self-proclaimed arbiters of "real news" spread misinformation like a virus, turning once-decentralized platforms, once safe havens from mainstream manipulation, into echo chambers of distortion. They're now paid big money to steer public attention away from systemic issues and toward controlled narratives that serve state power, corporate profits, and ideological obedience. This financial opportunity attracts more grifters selling misinformation polluting the journalism and media space and ultimately the public's mind.

Neo-fascism thrives in this environment.

- Nationalism and anti-intellectualism are sold as a "trendy" rebellion
- Censorship is reframed as "safety" and surveillance as "progress"
- Uses personal branding to bypass critique, reminiscent of authoritarian "strong man" optics. Repetition of empty rhetoric over debate. Billionaires are rebranded as heroes.

V. The Anatomy of Neo-Fascism

Neofascism is a process of creating illusory enemies, destroying public institutions, consolidating corporate + church & state power, glorifying strongmen, spreading disinformation and misogyny, replacing truth and equality with emotion, tradition, construct, and fear.

We see this play out in real time through:

- Firing civil servants, dismantling public institutions, and gutting regulation
- Transferring public wealth and assets into private hands through tax cuts, subsidies, and deregulation
- Stripping healthcare, education, housing, and social programs while expanding corporate welfare
- Weakening labor rights and making organizing harder or illegal
- Shielding corporations from lawsuits and public accountability
- Running government like a business instead of a public service
- Using media and memes as tools of mass behavior
- Distracting with culture wars to divide the public while consolidating power

This is where it all leads: a reality so distorted that civilian slaughter is framed as "defense," and anyone who questions it is labeled antisemitic, unpatriotic, or extremist. Through media gaslighting, algorithmic manipulation, and mass narrative control, the public has been conditioned to accept violence as necessary, dehumanize entire populations, and mistrust anyone who challenges state violence or tradition. The line between dissent and danger has been erased on purpose. We now live in a climate where questioning power is branded as terrorism, while actual hate is rebranded as being authentic to fill some unhealed psychological void. This is what fascism needs: not only obedience, but to prey on your confusion, inner turmoil, and moral disorientation. The oppressed are framed as the aggressors, and the perpetrators are portrayed as heroes. This propaganda becomes moral inversion, designed to paralyze action and fracture solidarity. It exploits history and identity to shield the empire from accountability. It creates a culture where morality and equality are punishable. This is the endgame of neofascist narrative control: not just to *OBEY*, but confusion so deep and disorientation so complete that the public cannot recognize an atrocity when it happens in front of them.

"Those who can make you believe absurdities can make you commit atrocities."- Voltaire

"We'll know our disinformation program is complete when everything the American public believes is false." – William J. Casey, Director of the CIA 1981-1987

I. JUSTICE: KNOW YOUR RIGHTS

LEGAL REBELLION IN A NEO-FASCIST STATE

This guide is your survival toolkit for defending both your rights and your autonomy in an era of creeping authoritarianism, it's vital to arm yourself with knowledge. Knowledge equals Power. Below, we break down major threats to democracy and civil liberties in the U.S. today, and how you can fight back legally.

The First Amendment of the U.S. Constitution explicitly protects the right to free speech, peaceful assembly, and protest. But in 30+ states, new laws turn sidewalks into crime scenes. You can now be arrested just for being nearby when someone else throws a bottle. Police charge "riot" by association. Protesters have been held on terrorism charges for standing in the wrong place.

Modern-day power brokers have unleashed a wave of anti-protest laws to criminalize protesters. Since 2017, dozens of state measures have dramatically increased penalties for protest-related offenses, often under the pretext of stopping "riots" or protecting infrastructure. All of these new anti-protest laws have been passed in states with authoritarian-leaning legislatures intent on chilling public outcry.

What this means: Peaceful protesters now risk felony charges for tactics that used to be minor offenses. For example, a 2020 Tennessee law makes it punishable by up to one year in jail simply for obstructing a street or sidewalk during a protest In Louisiana, protesting near a pipeline construction site can land you 5 years in prison for "trespassing." Florida's 2021 "anti-riot" law went so far as to make blocking traffic a felony, and it even grants civil immunity to vigilantes who drive their cars into crowds of protesters.

Stay informed of local laws: Research your state's protest laws (the ACLU and activist groups track these). Avoid tactics specifically criminalized or be prepared with legal support if you choose civil disobedience. For instance, if your state makes highway protests a felony, keep marches near sidewalks or designated routes to stay in the legal clear.

- Organize with legal observers: Have lawyers or trained legal observers on site. They can document police behavior and remind officers that the world is watching, which may deter abuses. If mass arrests happen, legal teams can invoke your rights quickly.
- Record everything: Video evidence is a powerful weapon. It's your First Amendment right to film police and public events. Document any provocation by

counter-protesters or police – this proof can defend you in court or turn the tables in the media. (Just be mindful: if you post footage, blur faces of fellow protesters to avoid aiding police surveillance.

- Use the buddy system: Never protest alone. Stick with comrades who can witness any interaction if police single you out. Agree on emergency contacts ahead of time. If someone is arrested, the others can call lawyers and press immediately.

You have the right to protest. Authoritarians want you to self-censor, don't. By knowing the new traps they've set (harsh penalties, vague "riot" definitions, anti-mask laws, etc.), you can protest on your own terms. Every time you legally outmaneuver their crackdown, you keep the spirit of resistance alive. The First Amendment is still on your side, and we must continue to exercise it defiantly yet shrewdly.

Know your rights: this not only protects you legally, but it also empowers you to assert control in the moment. Remember, the burden is on police to respect your rights, but in practice officers may not do so unless you hold the line.

Here's how to walk that line between standing up for yourself and staying safe:

Basic rights during any stop: You do NOT have to answer questions beyond identifying yourself (and in some states even that is not required)

Clearly state "I am exercising my right to remain silent"

You don't have to chit-chat about where you're going, what you're doing, or your political beliefs. If the police press, repeat your refusal calmly. Likewise, you do NOT have to consent to any search of yourself, your car, or your belongings

If an officer says, "mind if I look in your bag?" – you can and should say "No, I do not consent to a search." Even if they search anyway, your objection (said out loud) can help later in court to get any evidence thrown out.

Always remember silence is your shield. Anything you say can be used against you, so better to say nothing at all.

Police need probable cause to arrest. They cannot arrest you simply for being present. You can record the police in public.

Know your terrain. Stick to sidewalks and legal zones when available. Use legal observers. Mask up, it protects against facial recognition.

Loophole: if charged with a riot, check if there is any actual evidence of inciting violence. Passive presence is not incitement, demand full video review and challenge probable cause early.

Example: GEO-FENCED & TRACED – MINNESOTA

Scenario: Weeks after a protest, police show up claiming they have location data placing you at the scene.

What to do:

- Ask: "Do you have a warrant?"
- Do not confirm your location or identity verbally. Remain silent and ask for legal counsel.

Loophole: After George Floyd protests, police officers used geofence warrants to ID phones in protest zones. But these are legally shaky, and courts are starting to rule them unconstitutional. Don't self-incriminate. Let your lawyer or public defender challenge the data's validity.

II.   POLICE ENCOUNTERS: DON'T GET PLAYED

Police are trained to get you to talk. They'll pretend to be casual, that's the trap. You have the right to walk away if you're not detained. Ask directly: "Am I free to go?"

Say: "I do not consent." Say: "I want a lawyer."

Do not physically resist, they want you to escalate. But film everything. Ask for badge numbers. And the second you're cuffed: stop talking. Do not explain yourself. Do not try to reason. Do not sign anything.

Loophole: If they skip reading Miranda rights before questioning, your statements may be inadmissible. Invoke silence immediately to protect this.

III.   DIGITAL SELF-DEFENSE

Every smartphone is a surveillance device. Authorities use geofence warrants, scrape social feeds, track conversations, and apply facial recognition to identify and target organizers. Cops need a warrant to search your phone. You can refuse to unlock it, especially if it's passcode protected.

Use encrypted apps like Signal. Disable biometric logins.

Geofence warrants, social media monitoring, and facial recognition are real threats.

Before posting photos: scrub metadata. Avoid tagging others. Blur faces. Assume every app sells data to law enforcement.

During protests: use burner phones or airplane mode, or better yet leave it at home.

Loophole: Courts have ruled you can't be forced to reveal your passcode due to the Fifth Amendment. Don't install Face ID, they can physically force that.

IV. IMMIGRATION & ICE

ICE cannot enter your home without a judicial warrant signed by a judge. Most ICE agents only carry administrative warrants (Form I-200 or I-205), which do *not* give them legal authority to enter your home without permission. If you don't let them in, they cannot force entry without a signed judicial warrant. They'll bluff. Don't fall for it.

You do NOT have to open the door. You do NOT have to answer questions. You do NOT have to sign anything.

Say: "Slide the warrant under the door." Say: "I do not consent to entry." Say: "I am exercising my right to remain silent."

If they barge in: Do not resist. But state your objection clearly and try to document everything. You may have legal grounds to suppress the raid.

Do not sign a voluntary departure. Demand a hearing. If you fear persecution in your home country, say it out loud clearly. This can trigger asylum rights.

Have an emergency plan.

ICE cannot detain you based solely on a detainer request.

An ICE detainer (Form I-247) is not a warrant. It's a *request*, not an order. Local law enforcement agencies do not have to comply and in many cities they can't.

Loophole: If you've been in the U.S. for over two years, expedited removal likely does not apply. Know this and assert it.

Loophole: You are not required to carry ID as a non-citizen unless on a visa or green card. Do not lie, remain silent instead. Misrepresentation can void future protections.

Example: ICE AT WORKPLACE – ILLINOIS

Scenario: You're at your job in Chicago and someone yells "ICE!" Agents enter the building asking for IDs.

What to do: You have the right to remain silent and not show documents unless they present a judicial warrant with your name and judge's signature. Record everything.

Under the Fourth Amendment, ICE cannot legally enter a private, non-public area of a workplace without either a judicial warrant signed, or the consent of the employer or person in charge. Under the Illinois TRUST Act, police cannot detain you on an ICE hold without a warrant. If ICE doesn't show a judge-signed warrant, you and your employer can refuse cooperation legally. Document while recording, "They have no judicial warrant, and no one consented to entry." Make sure to give co-workers your family's number.

LEGAL ADVICE: ICE WON'T TELL YOU:

Your Rights: ICE can only hold you 72 hours without charges. Demand bond hearing immediately. Some violations have expiration dates. Government must prove illegal presence - you don't prove legal status. If questioned in custody, demand Miranda rights. Illegal searches void their evidence. You are allowed to have a free interpreter, to contact consulate, to review all evidence, appeal removal orders (know deadlines). Document Time/date, badge numbers, warrant status (photograph), rights violations, witnesses.

Ways to Fight Deportation:

Asylum: You can apply if you fear persecution in your home country.

Withholding of Removal: Stops deportation if you would face torture or violence if sent back.

Cancellation of Removal: If you've lived in the U.S. for over 10 years and your deportation would harm your U.S. citizen family, you may qualify for this relief.

V. WORKPLACE & POLITICAL RETALIATION

Most private employers can legally fire you for political speech. Exceptions exist, use them.

Know your state: Some protect off-duty speech, others don't. Public employees have more rights. If your activism is tied to workplace issues, labor law may protect you.

Say: "This is protected activity." Say: "I am engaging in speech on a matter of public concern."

Keep activism off work devices. Document retaliation. Public pressure can flip the power dynamic. Organize coworkers for collective protection.

Loophole: Link activism to workplace safety or discrimination concerns to invoke labor protections under the NLRA or Title VII.

V. WHISTLEBLOWING

Whistleblower laws protect you, but only if you follow proper channels. Free speech doesn't cover classified leaks. Agencies may retaliate or charge you with unrelated crimes. Report to Congress if needed. Understand protections within your agency. Expose corruption, not yourself.

If you leak to the press without using official channels, you can be prosecuted under the Espionage Act, even if what you exposed was true. Use whistleblower laws strategically: Report through Inspectors General or Congress. Use SecureDrop encrypted tips. Consult legal counsel before leaking. Document everything. Anticipate retaliation. Speak to watchdog orgs before going public.

Loophole: Whistleblowers reporting to Congress are protected by statute. Even intelligence employees have protected channels. Use them if possible.

VI. GENERAL SUMMARY STRATEGY: LOOPHOLES THAT RESIST

Ask: "Am I free to go?" If yes, walk away. If not, say nothing. Never consent to searches. Not your pockets. Not your bag. Not your car. Demand your lawyer. Do not talk. Do not sign anything without representation. Film cops. Record badge numbers. If arrested, invoke your rights and shut up.

Group solidarity protects you. Mass arrests often collapse when people don't self-incriminate.

Jury nullification exists; juries can refuse to convict if they see injustice. They just can't be told explicitly.

Know the system in your state or country. Use its contradictions and loopholes against it. Refuse to cooperate with your own repression.

If they pursue persecution the final step would be to File a Civil Rights Complaint

You can:

- File in federal court under 42 U.S.C. §1983 (a statute that lets you sue state actors for constitutional violations).
- File with the Department of Justice Civil Rights Division: https://civilrights.justice.gov/
- Consider Class Action or Partner with Groups

If others have experienced similar violations, this could become a class action case. Groups like the ACLU or NLG often take these on if the case has broader national implications. Use media and community pressure.

Your rights vary by state. Some states protect off-duty political activity. Public employees have more protections. Labor law shields organizing related to work conditions.

Say: "This is protected activity under [State Law / NLRA]." Say: "I am engaging in speech on a matter of public concern."

For Protest Arrests:

- Lawyers' Committee for Civil Rights Under Law: Offers legal support to individuals who have had their rights violated during protests or by ICE. Website: https://www.lawyerscommittee.org
- National Lawyers Guild (NLG): They have a network of attorneys who provide legal defense for activists and protesters. They often operate a legal observer program at protests. Website: https://www.nlg.org
- ACLU (American Civil Liberties Union): If your rights are violated during the arrest, the ACLU offers legal assistance and fights for civil liberties in protest-related cases. Website: https://www.aclu.org

2. For ICE Arrests:

- Immigrant Legal Resource Center (ILRC): Offers resources for immigrants facing ICE actions and provides legal referrals. Website: https://www.ilrc.org
- National Immigration Law Center (NILC): Provides legal help and advocacy for immigrants, especially regarding ICE raids and deportations. Website: https://www.nilc.org or https://unitedwedream.org

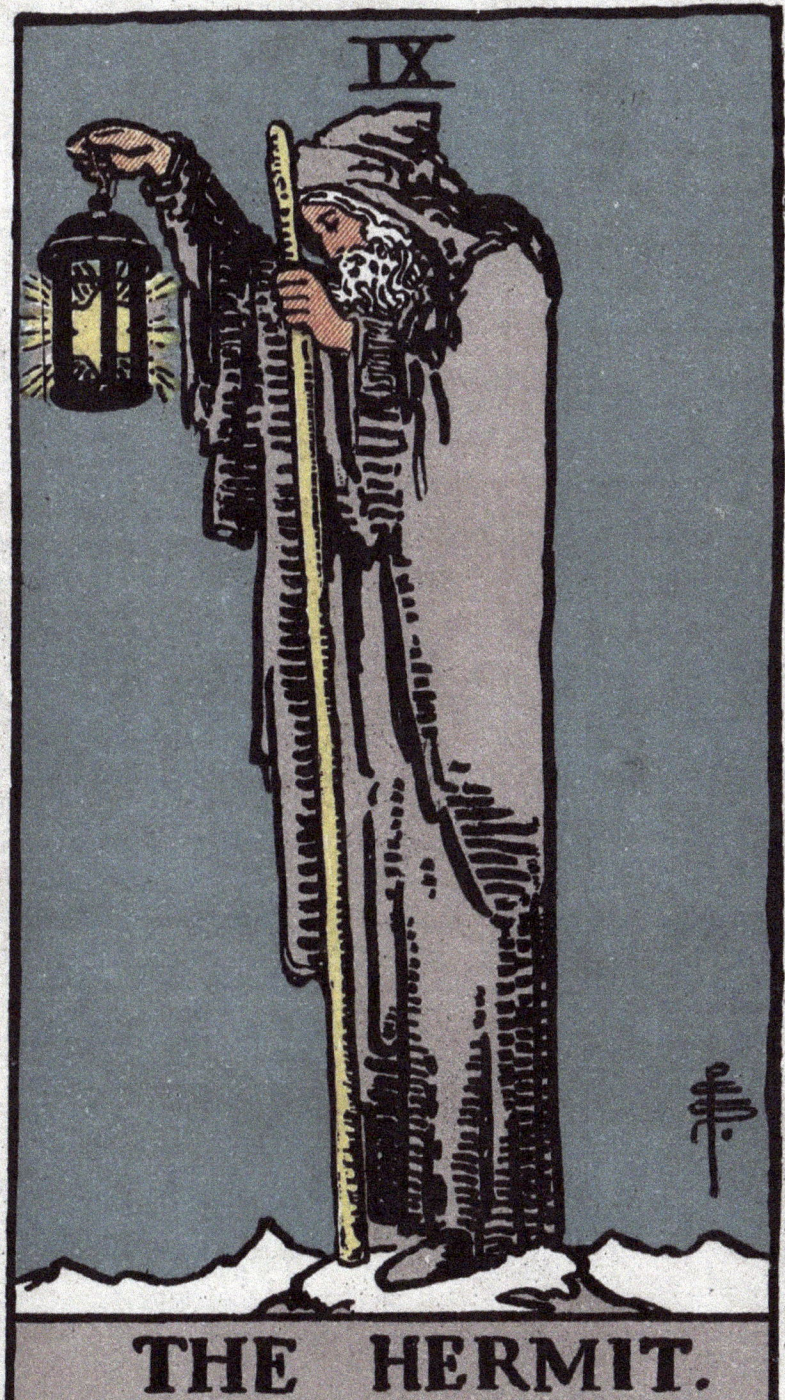

I. The Hermit: Know Thyself
Detaching from the Noise. Reconnecting to Intuition.

Modern day fascism thrives on emotional chaos: fear, outrage, tribalism, and unprocessed trauma. A population too emotionally dysregulated to think critically or connect across differences is easy to manipulate.

This is why reclaiming your inner awareness becomes a revolutionary act. The act of creating sacred withdrawal is not only for self-care, but also resistance. It's not about checking out. It's about opting out of the noise long enough to remember who you are beneath it. Withdrawal is a conscious disruption of the programming. So, you can move beneath reaction and groupthink, past the surface, and deep into the roots of intuition and presence. Into your actual values, not the ones you've been conditioned to perform.

It's about learning to reclaim your sovereignty. Before we can effectively unify and build a cohesive counterculture movement, we have to detox from the programming and the narratives. From the echo chambers and cognitive dissonance, and the trauma patterns, so we can learn who we are again beneath societal and parental conditioning. Fascist systems don't just dominate by means of policy and force; they dominate through psychology. Through memory and emotional reflex associated with unhealed trauma. It is a mind fuck, and the manipulation tactics from the manufactured consent playbook wreck the psyche and can turn us into something we aren't.

The system relies on your pain, your passion, your disorientation, and your longing for meaning to form bonds that feel empowering at first but keep you trapped. When people haven't healed, they confuse intensity for truth, familiarity for safety, and validation for justice. That's how movements that harm others start to feel like home. That's why someone will defend a leader who mirrors their inner rage, even if that leader upholds systems of violence. Because it doesn't feel like harm — it feels like validation for our experience, our trauma, and the parts we deny. It helps us to cope with our own brokenness. If certain leaders or movements awaken anger, righteousness, judgement, or belonging in us, it's worth asking what part of our pain or insecurity is being mirrored back. Only by understanding that reflection and story can we transform division into understanding and heal ourselves.

That's trauma bonding: when our unhealed wounds attach us to people, ideologies, or movements that replicate old dynamics, sometimes abusive ones, because they feel like home. Before we can think critically, we have to see clearly. And before we can see clearly, we have to understand *why* our trauma responses keep getting activated and manipulated.

Understanding Trauma Bonding: The Emotional Infrastructure of Control

Trauma bonding is not just a personal and collective issue; it's a political one. It is one of the most effective forms of control in modern society because it bypasses logic, bypasses values, critical thinking, and plugs directly into the dysregulated nervous system. It keeps individuals, and entire populations trapped in cycles of loyalty, fear, complacency, and misplaced trust. And fascism knows the battlefield is the nervous system. It knows people won't examine the roots of their reactions if it can keep them constantly *feeling triggered*. Angry. Vindicated. Afraid. Seen. Trauma bonding happens when the mind confuses harm with something meaningful, and direct intensity as what's right. It is rooted in our early psychological wiring:

- As children, many of us unfortunately learned to associate love with volatility or abandonment, attention with punishment, and identity/ego with survival. If your caregivers were inconsistent, controlling, or emotionally unsafe, your nervous system learned to attach anyway because attachment was essential to staying alive.
- As adults, we unconsciously reattach to that same pattern. This is the inner child's survival reflex, not conscious choice. We attract people, causes, and ideologies that reinforce these trauma patterns.
- At the ancestral level, we carry collective trauma: colonization, forced migration, slavery, genocide, abuse, imprisonment. These histories live in the body and DNA as hypervigilance, distrust, and fragmented identity. They make us susceptible to bonding with anything that recreates it or offers safety, certainty, or emotional validation, even if it's a trap, unhealthy, or even a good cause being co-opted.

Fascist systems found an opportunity to exploit this. They weaponize unresolved trauma by creating emotionally charged environments where people attach themselves to causes, figures, or ideologies not because they appear just or liberatory, but because they feel familiar, intense, or validating. Because they speak to an unhealed part of themselves. Judging and blaming others becomes a shortcut to regulating our own fear, shame, and uncertainty. It gives us a temporary illusion of control and moral superiority in a world where we feel powerless or unseen. So, the real question isn't just why we judge others. What are we avoiding in ourselves when we do? What pain are we outsourcing onto the world? What silence are we afraid to sit in? Healing interrupts that cycle. It dismantles the inner hooks that fascism and other extremist ideologies use to recruit and control.

Examples:

- Defending harmful leaders or ideologies because they seem to "speak your pain" often by offering a scapegoat or someone to blame. It becomes a way to avoid looking within or taking accountability. Even when their actions are oppressive, people may protect the very systems that harm them, mistaking oppression for acceptance.

- Latching onto a movement because it gives you validation and a sense of being in the "know," even if it reproduces abuse, hierarchy, or manipulation.
- Becoming addicted to political outrage cycles because they mirror unresolved chaos from our past and give you a false sense of purpose.
- Feeling loyalty to a community that shames, pressures, or isolates yourself or others, because we've internalized that control equals love and acceptance.

Trauma bonding isn't stupidity or weakness. It's a form of unprocessed survival code. And it will continue to hijack revolutionary energy and freedom until it is named, understood, and unraveled.

When the Wound Leads the Movement: Trauma Bonding Inside Resistance

Trauma bonding doesn't stop at mainstream culture or right-wing authoritarianism, it's just as present inside activist spaces, radical movements, and liberal communities. That's part of the trap: when people assume they've "done the work" because they're politically aligned, while still acting out unprocessed trauma in how they lead, organize, judge, and relate. You know the ego, the power trip, the vindictiveness, the rage, it's not just passion for the cause, it's a lack of internal emotional regulation. Unhealed trauma doesn't disappear when you put it in a collective, it scales and spreads. It reshapes entire movements in its glorified image. And that's how we get cult leaders.

Here's how trauma bonding shows up in resistance spaces:

- Leader fixation. Individuals get elevated into guru or savior roles, not because of mere strategy or wisdom, but because they mirror the community's pain, anger, or desire to be rescued. Critique becomes betrayal and accountability becomes an attack.
- Purity culture and cancellation. Spaces become obsessed with ideological perfection. One mistake, or perceived deviation leads to exile. This mimics childhood dynamics of conditional love and punitive environments. The community starts to feel like an emotionally abusive family system.
- Addiction to urgency creates trauma bonding through shared crisis. People stay in high-activation mode 24/7, protesting, doom scrolling, reacting to every crisis, refusing rest. Activism becomes trauma response. Slowing down feels like failure.

- False unity through shared pain. Movements often form around collective grief or rage, but without emotional intelligence, that shared trauma becomes the glue, and the limit. The second someone starts to heal and question or shift ideas; they're seen as disloyal or disconnected. We need to question everything.
- Shame as control. Instead of cultivating political maturity, shame becomes a mechanism for enforcing conformity. People are policed not for causing harm, but for failing to perform the correct trauma language, emotional displays, or ideological branding. Control is maintained through fear of mistake, not through constructive dialogue or growth. All of this serves authoritarian old paradigm systems. Why? Because it keeps movements reactive, fragile, and easy to dismantle from the inside. You don't need an external oppressor if people are already imploding under the weight of their own unresolved patterns within the container.

The system doesn't care if you call yourself radical, if your nervous system is still colonized, you're still controlled by someone or something.

Take back CONTROL. It's about saying: I will *not* give my nervous system to the system. I will not outsource my emotional energy to the news cycle, the algorithm, past abuse, or someone else's corrupt agenda. I will *feel* deeply but I will *respond* intentionally from a place of pure balanced resonance. This is the soil from which real unity and movement can grow.

Unity Without Sameness

Unity is not sameness. It is not an agreement on every point. It is not about merging into a hive mind. Real unity is shared clarity about the system, shared commitment to survival, and emotional maturity to stay in the fight together, even when it's uncomfortable and questions the status quo or biases. It's about holding each other accountable. Trauma bonding creates shallow, volatile unity. Emotional intelligence builds resilient, strategic unity.

We can hold different identities, perspectives, and wounds without tearing each other apart. But only if we've learned to regulate our nervous systems, interrogate our trauma patterns, and stay grounded in our shared values, not our triggers. We are all under psychological attack, and we have to help our fellow brothers and sisters out of the haze, while staying accountable for our own conditioning, if we are going to liberate from this predatory system.

II. Emotional Regulation in Practice: Strategic Grounding

Here are tangible steps to regulate your nervous system so you can stay clear, think critically, and show up with power:

1. Detach from constant stimulation. Log off of all devices. Mute. Take 24 hours in silence.
2. Move your body. Trauma gets stuck in stillness. Walk, stretch, dance, shake. Regulate physically first then emotionally through meditation or breathwork.
3. Feel without spiraling and without shame. Give yourself space to cry, rage, or grieve without fusing to those states. Let emotions move through you, not define you, and know it's ok to feel intensely just process it safely.
4. Reconnect with your intuition. Once the noise quiets, you'll feel your own voice again. Not your fear. Not your conditioning. Not that voice running nonstop in your head that's not you. The observer, the calm beyond that storm.
5. Pause before reacting to potential conflict. Every time. Walk away for a period. Reactions are too easy. Regulation is intentional and patient.
6. Practice discernment. Ask: Is this my truth, or my trauma? Is this solidarity, or enmeshment? Is this justice, or control? Is this ego or my true self? Practicing awareness builds healthy regulation.

Tactical Nervous System Defense

Regulation is a discipline. It's how we take control back from the systems that depend on our burnout, confusion, and collapse.

1. **Activate or Tone the Vagus Nerve**
   The vagus nerve is the command center of your parasympathetic nervous system, your body's "rest and restore" switch. When damaged you are constantly in "fight of flight" mode. When activated, it signals safety to your brain and body. You can't think critically or build strategy while your body thinks you're under threat.

Developed by Stanley Rosenberg, this exercise targets the Vagus nerve:

- Lie on your back and interlace your fingers behind your head.
- Without turning your head, look to the right as far as possible with your eyes.
- Hold this position until you yawn or sigh, then repeat on the left side. Do this several times until you feel complete.

The vagus nerve runs along the carotid sheath on either side of the neck:

- Apply light pressure with your thumb just below the ear, moving down towards the collarbone.
- Use gentle, upward strokes along the side of the neck.

2. **Breathwork: Rewire from Survival Mode**
   Your breath is the most accessible tool for interrupting panic, anxiety, or reactivity. Try this: Box Breathing (used by special forces and trauma therapists 4- 7 secs): Inhale for 7 seconds → Hold for 7 → Exhale for 7→ Hold for 7 → Repeat for 3–5 mins. This builds regulation and authority over your state.

3. **Somatic Awareness: Get Out of Your Head, Into Your Body**
   You're not going to think your way out of trauma, your body and cells store the memory. Regulation begins with embodiment.
   - Do a body scan through quiet observation. Where are you clenched, bracing, numb?
   - Move. Shake your arms. Tap your chest. Stomp your feet. Move until you feel a shift.
   - Orient. Look around the room slowly. Name what you see. This reminds your brain you are here now, not in the past. Now tune into how you feel in the body, in the mind, in the emotion, process it, honor it, and then shake or dance it off. Then to close put your hands on your heart and visualize something that makes you feel very happy, safe, and appreciated.

4. **Joy, Creativity, laughter, and Play Are Not Optional**
   Fascism feeds on despair so starve it. This is our nervous system's medicine. Joy, art, movement, dance, laughter interrupt the cycle of dysregulation and reclaim your vitality.

5. **Boundaries Are Regulation Tools**
   Psychic boundaries are not selfish, they're strategic. You are not meant to consume every piece of bad news. You are not required to fight every battle. You can't liberate others if you're perpetually depleted by media and energy vampires.

Try:
   - Mute or unfollow outrage cycles.
   - Exit conversations that spiral into fear or purity performance.
   - Say "not right now. I need space" and mean it.
   - Surround yourself and give your time to those you admire and uplift you

6. **Remember: Clarity Is the Goal, Not Numbness or Avoidance**
   Regulation is the ability to *feel everything* without being controlled by any of it. To be aware of the nature of feeling and to lean into it to process and heal. To not let it control you. You can feel grief, rage, betrayal, fear and still act from wisdom knowing this feeling is not who you are but a small transitory aspect of being human.

Emotional Regulation Enables Strategic Unity

Once you've regulated, you can think again. And not just for yourself, for the collective. This is where emotional regulation turns into the realest and strongest threat to fascism: people who are emotionally clear, strategically aligned, and united have the foundation for a successful resistance. Fascism needs people too triggered to recognize strategic propaganda, too divided to build coalitions, too exhausted to plan beyond the next resistance cycle.

Upgrade your Mindset:

- Critical thinking allows you to challenge narratives and see beyond propaganda.
- Systems thinking helps you understand patterns of power and design interventions that matter.
- Collective sense-makings skills allows you to build shared reality and solutions by breaking down illusions and falsehoods in a time of disinformation and confusion.
- Emotional intelligence keeps you grounded so you can hold space for disagreement, complexity, and evolving understanding.

III. Historical Precedents: Unity Under Pressure

The French Resistance under Nazi occupation was not ideologically unified. It was a patchwork of communists, Catholics, socialists, anarchists, former conservatives, and students. What united them wasn't perfect agreement, it was awareness of danger. They developed decentralized cells to avoid collapse, used collective sense-making to identify threats, and built underground networks through shared purpose. They didn't wait for perfect alignment. They acted with strategic compassion and disciplined intelligibility to be successful.

The Civil Rights Movement, from the NAACP's legal battles to the student-led direct actions of SNCC and the revolutionary impact of the Black liberation movements, was genius activism and one of the strongest movements of all time. Within the nonviolent wing, emotional regulation was tactical. Activists trained under organizers like James Lawson and Diane Nash to remain calm through arrest, harassment, and assault. Workshops taught them to master fear and suppress reactive instincts, to hold moral ground without flinching and stay unified under pressure and within organizing.

The Zapatistas in Chiapas, the Polish Solidarity movement, and anti-Apartheid coalitions in South Africa, all built unity across class, identity, and ideology because they were rooted in a shared vision. They prioritized what mattered: autonomy, dignity, liberation. These movements practiced emotional regulation as a survival skill: patience under state violence, restraint when provoked, empathy across cultural divides and in collaboration.

IV. Regulated Empathy: The Path to Compassionate Strategy

We don't need to agree on everything to find common ground. We only need emotional maturity, paired with the ability to sit in discomfort, to hold disagreement, to choose emotional neutrality over individual justification. Non-violent communication practices should be a part of every group's personal and collective ethos.

This is regulated empathy:

- Seeing someone's pain without absorbing it.
- Listening to disagreement without personalizing it.
- Offering compassion without losing discernment.
- Speaking truth without shaming.

Without this, we get ego wars disguised as politics. An ideological silos where everyone sounds the same and nothing evolves and internal collapse again. More of the same failed movement. If we stay divided over trauma, purity, or identity performance, we lose. Period.

Fascist leaning wings win when we splinter over language, accuse each other over tone, exile each other over imperfection or ideology, and forget that we are being played by the same machine. You can be different and still be aligned morally.

The question is not "Do I agree with them on everything?"

The question is: "Are they fighting the same hidden enemy? Are they fighting systems of domination, not just symptoms? Are they working toward a world where no one is disposable?

If the answer is yes: expose the root and collaborate.

I. The Magician: Taking Back Your Power

Reclaiming your power starts with a confrontation of self. It's the process Jung called individuation: meeting the parts of yourself you've exiled, reclaiming them, and allowing the whole psyche to speak from a healed place. Next is to address the social constructs, gender roles, economic status, race hierarchies, religious dogma, and societal definitions of "normal" and "success." These tools of control have kept our true being suppressed. From the moment we're born, we're conditioned to obey systems that do not serve our personal liberation: education that promotes compliance over critical thought, religion that punishes opposition and deflects from doing the inner work, media that manufactures perception and distorts worth, and a state that punishes autonomy. This is a part of the scarcity conditioning to keeps us locked into a hidden societal program that keeps us dependent on their system and fearful of true liberation.

The Magician archetype exists to expose the illusion and remind you that your capacity to think for yourself, create, and resist was always within. The Magician reclaims that connection to the raw, direct, unfiltered experience of reality. This is the biological, energetic, and perceptual intelligence that keeps you grounded in what's truly real, not what's manufactured.

Once Attuned:

- You question everything. You do not accept "normal" or the general consensus as truth. You do not accept absolutes, even from your own side. You know truth is subjective and shifts depending on who's holding it and bias is hidden in all of us.
- You refuse to outsource thinking. You see the bigger picture, and not just one scene, through institutional narratives, algorithmic manipulation, sensationalism, and identity-based control.
- You reconnect to the field of life around you. Nature, breath, movement, sensation, silence.
- You unlearn obedience and oppression. You relearn rebellion for justice, healing for freedom.

II. Spiritual Rebellion Has Always Been Part of the Fight

This is not new. Throughout history, people have resisted fascism not just with weapons and physical force, but with their mind and spirit.

Leo Tolstoy promoted Christian anarchism: rejecting state violence, private property, and religious institutions, advocating instead for radical nonviolence, self-governance, and ethical autonomy.

Emma Goldman fused anarchism with emotional and spiritual freedom, championing reproductive rights, free love, and the rejection of religious and moral codes that bound women and workers to obedience.

The CNT-FAI in Spain, during the Spanish Civil War, fought fascism through collectivized farms, worker-run schools, and a complete rejection of Church-State power. They built decentralized systems of living and belief as a tactical rejection of Catholic-authoritarian rule.

The Liberation Theology Movement (1960s–1980s, Latin America)

Faced with brutal U.S.-backed regimes, Catholic priests, and revolutionaries in countries like El Salvador, Brazil, and Nicaragua harnessed faith to mobilize the working class and poor against fascism and capitalist violence.

- Liberation theologians interpreted scripture through the lens of Marxist class analysis, positioning Jesus as a revolutionary figure of the oppressed.
- Base communities, small, self-governed spiritual study circles, became sites of radical education, political organizing, and mutual aid.
- The Vatican and U.S. intelligence labeled them dangerous. Many were surveilled, assassinated, or disappeared, because they successfully united spiritual meaning with class consciousness and rebellion versus using faith to install fear and obedience.

III. Counterculture as Strategic Rejection (1960s–1980s)

The hippie and punk movements are often misrepresented as aesthetic or escapist. In reality, they were tactical counterattacks on the mind-control systems of Cold War America and late-stage industrial capitalism.

- Hippies rejected post war conformity, consumerism, and militarism. They used psychedelics to break perceptual conditioning and become more multi-dimensional. They built communes, alternative schools, and free clinics. Many were directly involved in anti-war and allies with Black liberation organizing.
- Punk movements (UK and US) explicitly resisted fascism, corporate media, and nationalist narratives. DIY culture was not just style; it was a direct assault on capitalist production and cultural control. Bands like Crass embedded anarchist philosophy into sound, visuals, and direct-action making art as a protest.

Black Power and Political Resistance

- The Black Panther Party embraced self-determination not just materially (free breakfast, clinics, education) but also ideologically, rejecting white supremacist Christianity and colonial morality. Figures like Huey Newton explored existentialism and psychology as tools of internal liberation.
- The Rainbow Coalition (founded by Fred Hampton) united Black, Brown, and poor white communities across cultural lines, not through sameness, but shared political education and mutual respect. It drew on spiritual frameworks of dignity and collective destiny that stood in direct opposition to white capitalist individualism.
- The Nation of Islam, the Five Percenters, and Rastafarian movements redefined God, history, and power, rooting Black spiritual identity in resistance, not subjugation. These were counter-theologies built to reclaim narrative control and reject white hegemony in both the church and the state.

These movements and free thinkers created parallel cultures that challenged the legitimacy of the dominant one understood. They understood what The Magician embodies: Spiritual decolonization is necessary for strategic resistance against control and hypocrisy. To fight fascism externally, you must first dismantle the narratives embedded in your perception, memory, and inherited identity.

IV. What Is Spiritual Anarchy?

Spiritual Anarchy is the rejection of systems that colonize spirituality to define you. It is the refusal of any imposed belief system — religious, capitalist, nationalist, or moral — used to control behavior, manufacture consent, or regulate identity. It's not about "finding your truth," it's about refusing the default narratives we were programmed to accept. It's about reclaiming an authentic interconnection with the universe and all inhabitants of Earth. Honoring that we are a part of the web of life that predates and will outlast every system trying to own you.

Spiritual Anarchy = internal autonomy + external disobedience. The reclamation of thought, perception, and value creation from institutions that want your soul domesticated. In this crisis of consciousness, the system has hijacked our true nature, and our connection to the subtle energies that govern our universe.

What it looks like:

- Rejecting the aspects of religion as a tool of social control, without having to reject its meaning, faith, interconnection, spirituality, ethics, or mystery if you don't want to.
- Reclaiming connection to not only your own inner presence, but to land, body, ancestors, and the greater unknown on your own terms.

- Refusing to moralize struggle, genocide, obedience, or suffering.
- Refusing systems that reward spiritual performance and obedience but punish freedom of thought and liberation.
- Building values and systems that serve people, and planet not institutions or profit.

Spiritual Anarchy says: you do not owe your mind, your spirit, or your values to an empire. Not the state. Not capitalism. Not organized religion, nor culture. That is yours alone to discover and liberate. You are not here to fit in. You are not here to comply. You are here to break the cycle of societal conditioning to be free again.

What Spiritual Anarchy is *Not*:

- New Age escapism – commodified spirituality repackaged for individualism and profit.
- Spiritual bypassing – using "love and light," detachment, or positive vibes only to avoid reality, dismiss oppression, or bypass your own trauma and conflict.
- Instagram enlightenment – performative depth, aestheticized suffering, and algorithm-approved "truth."
- Ritual consumerism – turning ancestral or esoteric knowledge and practices into wellness capitalism branding.
- Vibe-based politics – replacing critical thinking with emotional reaction, cognitive dissonance, or trending aesthetic alignment.

To reclaim your power is to move out of scarcity and into abundance, away from individualism and toward interconnection, letting indoctrinated constructs fall away so consciousness can expand. It's a reformation of your innate connection to the universe and all living things, a return to what you were before they trained you to forget. Remember the true nature of being a conscious mind, and act accordingly from the higher self and being heart-centered looks like this:

- You understand how your thoughts, values, and fears were shaped by others & ego, and consciously reject what doesn't serve the highest good or respect all life.
- You engage with reality *as it is* beyond the noise, not through state narratives, cultural mythologies, or algorithmic echo chambers.
- You reclaim the right to define meaning, ethics, and truth for yourself, rooted in interdependence and systemic awareness.
- You recognize your connection to all living systems, not as a belief, but as a biological, spiritual, and political reality. This is psychological demilitarization.

You are the magician of your life, here to transmute trauma into wisdom, suffering into purpose, and chaos into creative liberation. Spirituality doesn't have to mean indoctrination or new age woo. It's about the direct awareness of the underlying, quantum nature of reality and ourselves.

I. The Empress- Building A Movement

Resisting Oppression by Remembering the Sacred. Fascism, like all systems of control, survives by severing our lines of connection — to nature, instinct, each other, and to truth. When people are cut off from what exists outside the consumer world, they're easier to rule. The counterworld begins with remembrance. Indigenous knowledge. Regenerative systems and models that are rooted in reciprocity and organizing that restores balance and builds community. We've been divided for so long that the loneliness has become lethal to our ancestral role as primarily communal beings.

The Empress is the version of you that exists outside the matrix, the part that's connected to the real world, the natural world, and everything you can't see but still feel. She trusts the intelligence of life itself, not the man-made systems built on domination and scarcity. The Empress doesn't play by those rules. She refuses to participate in a system built on domination, scarcity, and control. She is the nurturer, plants, builds, protects, divests, and heals. To regenerate the earth is to rebel against every system that profits off of extraction.

Purity Over Scale: How Movements Collapse

Most organizations collapse before they're defeated. The cause is internal contraction. As their movement expands, moral coherence overshadows progress. The demand for ideological purity replaces inclusivity which is required to scale. This phenomenon, what sociologists call boundary hardening: creates symbolic unity at the cost of strategic capacity. The issue is not the values themselves but how they are misused as a projection of our own inner turmoil.

What it looks like:

- Movements often ask participants to use precise language and engage through specific frameworks: such as trauma theory, decolonial rhetoric, or abolitionist semantics. This practice encourages mindfulness and solidarity, but it can also feel alienating to those who don't yet speak that language fluently or who are still learning how to navigate these evolving frameworks. Education and compassion is replaced with public shaming and canceling.
- Activists often spend more time policing each other than organizing against actual systems of oppression.
- Strategy is replaced with empty ideals and performative virtue, where real action is overshadowed by these surface-level gestures and soapbox media.
- Inside fracturing under the weight of interpersonal conflict, self-righteous leaders, moral superiority, and projections.

Fascists exploit purity culture by:
- Infiltrating and triggering internal collapse
- Amplifying internal drama to discredit the movement externally
- Using identity confusion and reactionary backlash to redirect potential allies into their pipelines

Why Movements Fail
- **No shared strategy or clear intent:** Fragmented campaigns chase different goals with no common timeline or coordination.
- **Symbolic politics:** Awareness replaces action; "raising visibility and trending" becomes the endpoint with no clear long-term strategy nothing changes.
- **Organizational isolation:** Each group operates alone, no cross-pollination collaboration, no weaving of shared mobilization, logistics, or messaging. We need a powerful decentralized solidarity network, not just one organization trying to plan broken-up actions.
- **Poor narrative strategy:** The opposition still controls the story. Movements ignore marketing, leaving the mass psychology tactics to elitists and corporations.
- **Unclear escalation paths:** Protests with no follow-through or clear direction or action dissipate energy instead of building on the momentum.
- **Digital dependence:** Reliance on algorithms and closed platforms leads to censorship, data exposure, and co-optation.

Historical Comparison:

The Black Panther Party and other 1960s–70s revolutionary organizations explicitly rejected purity culture. They brought in people from different backgrounds, including ex-gang members, white allies, independents, and veterans, if they were committed to action and willing to be trained in political education and discipline. They only required people to show up and do the work. Movements fail when they centralize power. The most effective recent model of decentralized, bottom-up resistance is the Zapatista Movement in Chiapas, Mexico (1994–present).

Why it works:
- No single leader = no easy takedown
- Autonomous local councils = local control over land, education, and health
- Resistance paired with reconstruction: they didn't just protest, they built new systems
- Anti-capitalist, Earth-centered without becoming a cult or a brand

What this means for us: Stop waiting for a unifying leader. Organize in small, autonomous cells that can **operate independently** but **organize collectively**.

Each cell should have four functions:
- a survival function (food, water, shelter, med, etc...provided)
- a communication channel (zines, decentralized network, secure chat)
- a political education practice and direct-action base (study groups, strategy organizing, skill shares)
- a regeneration function (garden, seed bank, trauma circles, mutual aid distro). The goal is mass viability. Start small and local then expand.

II. Anti-Fascist Movement Starter Checklist

How to Start a Real Movement (Not a Brand or Cult)

1.Start with a Shared Threat + Material Conditions

A real movement isn't built around identity. It starts with people who are:

Affected by the same system (policing, prejudice, food and water scarcity, climate collapse, censorship, fascism etc.) Ready to organize around that shared material threat (not just discourse but with real solutions and direct coordinated civil action.)

Build Political Clarity

People need to know what the hell you're fighting and why. Otherwise, it's chaos. It can't be so broad. Movements collapse when they try to fight everything at once. Political clarity means narrowing your focus until action becomes possible. If fascism is the structure, identify one mechanism that sustains it, like corporate donors funding extremist candidates, tech platforms enabling surveillance, media empires that amplify hate, and concentrate pressure there. People are most inspired by achievable disruption. Define what impact looks like, communicate it clearly, and make every message, post, or protest point back to that concrete goal. Without focus, movements dissolve after momentum dies. With it, they become a force. For example: Identify what fascism looks like in your local context: Host a political education group to find your cell. Discuss: Who benefits from fascism? How does capitalism sustain it? What institutions must fall? Avoid purity tests. Educate, don't exile or react.

2.Form an Organizing Core: Codify Culture: Behavior, Boundaries, and Vision

- Recruit 3-10 people who are grounded, ready to take action, and ready to build.

- Set roles: internal communications, logistics, content, organizing, outreach, mutual aid, safety, and education. A group without structure will default to hierarchy, so build a flat model from the start. Focus on collective leadership, where each member's contribution is valued. This avoids creating ego-driven dynamics and ensures that everyone feels invested in the success of the project. Eventually every role should have a backup person, every decision documented, every skill cross-trained.
- Create a Strong Ethos: Develop a shared ethos or guiding principles that define how the group operates. This can include a manifesto, a set of agreements, or a code of conduct. The goal is to maintain a culture free of drama, trauma, and projection, so that discussions remain productive and focused on the agreed upon mission and action. Use encrypted tools but also schedule offline intervals. Meet physically when possible. Train members in operational privacy and narrative security. Create an emergency action protocol: what if someone is doxxed, arrested, hacked? Make a printed and digital People's Guide: know your rights, manifesto, safe resources, contact info, direct action, and strategy goals.
- Regular Check-Ins and Self-Reflection: Draft a short manifesto or shared agreements that define how the group operates and resolves conflict. Schedule separate time and space for interpersonal conflicts and emotional processing – never let personal issues derail strategy meetings or action planning. Conflict doesn't always destroy movements, avoidance and ego's do.
- Foster a Culture of Accountability: Create systems for mutual accountability where members in council style support each other's growth and challenge harmful behaviors without fostering a culture of blame. This ensures that the group remains focused on collective improvement and maintains integrity in action. Use consensus or modified consensus to make decisions. Discipline is what keeps non-hierarchical structures from imploding.

3.Mobilize Your Community and Gain Support Through Being in Service: Start where people feel the system's depravity the most: food, housing, health access, safety. First events should feel like community, not just aid or recruitment. Music, food, art, and great story-sharing, & emotion builds solidarity and recruits. Example: Create mobile food stations that respond to local needs or build a community garden. **Launch day:** Host a block party, free workshop, or community meal. Invite an action: Every event should have a next step, sign up, bring supplies, join a crew, do outreach.

Services to Offer: Emergency Legal Defense Networks: Expand beyond bail funds to include rapid-response legal aid and legal clouds, support for deportation defense, and advocacy for workers' rights in immediate crisis situations. Form street teams that respond to evictions, police stops, ICE raids, or workplace exploitation.

Cultural Centers and Gathering Spaces: The camps at Standing Rock were not just about resistance; they were about creating a cultural space for ceremony, community-building, and solidarity. Reclaim public or donated spaces as hubs for collective healing and organizing. Community art walls, teach-ins, vigils, ceremony, film nights, clinics, childcare, shelter, clothing swap, whatever your community needs. Think "civic operating bases." Each hub should host three continuous functions: skills exchange, cultural production, and resource coordination. Link them through physical bulletin boards and digital mirrors (Matrix or Mastodon servers).

Counter-Surveillance: Replace isolated security workshops with community digital militias. Teach not just encryption but data minimalism, metadata hygiene, and narrative defense, how to resist manipulation and deepfake propaganda. Treat media literacy as counter-intelligence training.

Sovereignty Training: Guide communities to reclaim autonomy by teaching them to cultivate their own food systems, economic independence, decentralization, establish independent communication networks, and practice self-governance rooted in ancestral knowledge. Pair Resistance with Regeneration: Build food forests, community kitchens, tool shares, and co-living housing. People still depend on old paradigm systems for convenience; we have to recreate them: childcare networks, resource swaps, and time banks. Make art and music that reflects the world you're building and build a community around it to mobilize.

Run Targeted Disruption and Reverse Propaganda: Using storytelling, memes, and visual culture to subvert corporate and state messaging in a positive framing. Use humor, aesthetics, and emotional dissonance to shift perception. Every poster, meme, or slogan should either clarify power or parody it until it loses legitimacy. As sociologist Dylan Riley observed, fascism and revolution both grow from civic foundations, the networks people already belong to. That's the missing layer. Rebuild civic life as infrastructure for resistance. The most radical thing we can do is make community functional again, not only for survival but for disruption and change. Political scientist Sidney Tarrow called successful movements "cycles of contention," waves that build, peak, institutionalize, then adapt before repression sets in. Each wave must hit where the system is weakest, not only where emotion is highest.

Start with power mapping: chart who funds what, who enforces what, and who controls the narrative. Trace the links between corporate donors, media channels, and political offices. Identify five core domains of control: finance, logistics, technology, law, and legitimacy. Every action, boycott, leak, protest, or campaign, should target at least one. Disruption without analysis only feeds the spectacle. Build distributed intelligence networks: researchers, data analysts, storytellers, and legal observers operating in sync. This is your civic intelligence, a form of collective counter-surveillance that rivals state capacity. Use open-source investigation methods, trace lobbying flows, and publish transparent dossiers that expose connections between power centers.

Next, plan escalation cycles. Each begins with public education, moves to direct disruption, then transitions into structural replacement. For example: expose a bank's ties to detention centers, organize a divestment campaign, then open or partner with a community credit union or cooperative lending circle. Every confrontation must build an alternative, otherwise it only reinforces dependency on the old order. Use networked escalation, multiple nodes acting on shared goals across cities. Think of it as a supply chain of resistance: researchers feed organizers, organizers feed media teams, media feeds narrative, narrative recruits new action. Each part sustains the others.

Movement Building Checklist:

1. Disrupt Core Systems of Power: Target the foundations of fascist and neoliberal control by organizing actions that disrupt the functioning of key financial institutions, extractive industries, or government agencies that perpetuate systemic violence and inequality. This includes redirecting the flow of capital, targeting tax havens, or focusing on industries that profit off of human suffering, like private prison economies, universities investing in weapons manufacturers, banks funding pipelines, insurance companies covering corporations and militarized policing.

2. Subvert the Narrative of Fear: Counter the mainstream media's fascist-friendly narratives by creating alternative media platforms and groups that amplify resistance voices, stories of survival, and expose the contradictions of those in power. Use guerrilla tactics such as viral campaigns, independent reporting, and flooding their comment sections with truth to undermine the media machine that perpetuates corporate and fascist control.

3. Reclaim Strategic Locations: Peacefully assemble near spaces of state or corporate power, like government buildings, ICE offices, corporate headquarters, or predatory lender offices, and transform them into hubs for resistance and community support. These actions disrupt normal operations and draw attention to injustices while providing resources, education, and solidarity.

4. Defund and Deconstruct Corporate Influence: Move beyond calls for corporate accountability and focus on dismantling the financial systems that support fascist policies. This could involve organizing mass divestment campaigns, coordinated account closures from complicit banks, boycotting industries that fund hate and control, and targeting pension funds investing in private prisons and venture capital funding surveillance tech.

5. Create New Paradigm Models: Start local. Build community-based infrastructure that challenges the power of the state and corporate monopolies: worker-led cooperatives, mom and pop shops, autonomous zones that model self-governance, and mutual-aid networks that meet daily needs faster than institutions. Form neighborhood councils capable of rapid mobilization, organizing petitions, recall votes, and ballot initiatives that push policy within weeks, not years. Leverage local media, public records, and town halls to expose corruption and coordinate pressure campaigns on officials.

6. Disrupt through Culture and Art: Use culture as a tool for direct action. Art, music, performance, flash mobs that expose corporate crimes, guerrilla theater that dramatizes systemic violence, and murals that rewrite history on public walls can serve as powerful tools to disrupt fascist narratives and shift public consciousness. Mobilize collective creativity and artists to subvert power structures by disrupting public events, influencing cultural discourse, and fostering mass collective rebellion. Take a notes from the punk-rock era and transcendentalists and form a new thought movement.

Think of your activism as part of a vast, interconnected organism, where each cell plays a vital role. Just as cells in a body exchange resources to keep the whole system functioning, activist groups must share knowledge, support, and resources to create a powerful unified force.

Identify Common Ground: Find shared goals and values to unite diverse groups.

- **Respect Autonomy:** Honor individual freedoms and self-determination within the collective.
- **Build Consensus**: Foster collaborative decision-making where everyone's voice is heard and valued.
- **Cross-Pollinate Strategies and Tactics:** Hold joint strategy sessions where different activist groups can present their unique approaches, learn from one another, and adapt strategies that complement each other. For example, a group focused on racial justice may share community-building tactics with environmental activists, while mutual aid groups can provide logistical support to frontline protesters.
- **Organize Multi-Issue Campaigns:** Design campaigns that tackle multiple correlated issues at once, like a campaign that focuses on both worker exploitation

and environmental degradation from the same company. This way, different groups contribute to a single, focused action that impacts a range of targets. For example, pressuring a factory's supply chain might address labor exploitation and environmental harm simultaneously, creating broader disruption. Plan actions that target interconnected systems. By using strategic timing and collective power, these disruptions can cause greater systemic shake-ups, forcing a larger shift in policy or public attention.

- **Building a Resource Pool:** Create a shared pool of resources, whether that's materials for protests, people power for events, or financial support, that all groups can resource share. By pooling resources, your collective impact multiplies, and the burden on each group is reduced, allowing for more strategic and effective actions.
- **Mapping:** Before building coalitions, map who has decision-making power in your target systems. Identify which officials, corporate boards, or institutions can actually change policies. Then build coalitions specifically designed to hit those exact pressure points.
- **Opposition Research:** Study how your enemies coordinate against you. Corporate lobbying groups share strategies, police departments coordinate surveillance, and right-wing groups cross-train. Learn their coordination methods and adapt them for resistance.

III. Boycott as Direct Action: How to Cancel Fascism by Cutting Off Its Funding

The system at whole is propped up by corporations, banks, defense contractors, and tech platforms. These institutions provide the logistics, funding, and infrastructure that make authoritarianism scalable. They are not neutral, and they are not untouchable.

Historically, economic resistance has been one of the most effective forms of collective sabotage. From the Montgomery Bus Boycott in 1955–56 to global sanctions against apartheid South Africa, strategic boycotts have undermined regimes and forced change.

Step 1: Identify the Target

The most effective targets are companies with deep ties to state power, fascist regimes, and systemic violence. Look for those profiting from surveillance, militarism, labor exploitation, environmental destruction, and cultural control.

Key targets in the current corporate-fascist landscape:

- Amazon – Contracts with DHS, ICE, and police for surveillance tech; crushes labor organizing; monopolizes logistics and supply chains.
- BlackRock / Vanguard / State Street – Major shareholders in arms manufacturers, fossil fuels, private prisons, and companies involved in Israeli apartheid.
- Raytheon / Lockheed Martin / Boeing – Produce weapons used in war, occupation, and state violence worldwide.
- Nestlé – Profits from water privatization, child labor in cocoa supply chains, and domination of global food markets.
- Google (Alphabet) / Meta (Facebook, Instagram) – Operate global surveillance and data extraction systems; enable censorship and algorithmic manipulation. Technocratic authoritarianism, mass surveillance, and behavioral control through data infrastructure. Provides infrastructure that amplifies far-right networks.
- Walmart / Target – Dominate rural retail and food access; drive out small businesses; exploit workers and suppress wages.
- Chevron and Exxon – Responsible for major oil spills, environmental devastation, and corporate-backed violence against frontline communities.

Step 2: Define the Strategy

A boycott isn't just "don't buy." It's about disrupting profits, legitimacy, and logistics. That means coordinating mass action over time, amplifying the message, and offering people real alternatives.

To do damage, a boycott must:

- Be sustained: at least 3 months of organized pressure
- Be visible: the target must know why they're being hit
- Be replicable: easy for others to adopt in other cities or online
- Be disruptive: it must cause loss, revenue, reputation, control

Step 3: Organize the Phases and Create Your Campaign

Here's a clear boycott timeline with escalated phases:

Weeks 1–2: Educate + Recruit +Conscious Propaganda

- Launch teach-ins, flyers, zine drops, social infographics, hashtags, memes, viral videos, and influencer power.
- Explain why this company is corrupt

- Host discussions on surveillance capitalism, authoritarian connection, colonial supply chains, or military contracts.

Weeks 3-6: Mass Exit + Refusal

- Coordinate cancellations: accounts, subscriptions, apps, payments
- Help people switch to alternatives: food co-ops, encrypted tools, local markets
- Encourage economic refusal: no delivery, no contracts, no brand loyalty

Weeks 7-10: Disrupt Logistics + Profit Flow

- Organize warehouse blockades, city contract challenges, campus pressure campaigns
- Expose internal records, worker testimonies, unethical practices
- Make it unprofitable and politically messy to be associated with the target

Weeks 11-16+: Escalate or Sustain

- Move into physical disruption: walkouts, occupations, contract strikes
- Target investors, supporters, city councils, or major clients
- Connect to other movements: workers' rights, environmental justice, anti-surveillance

Step 4: Replace What You Remove

Most boycotts fail because they don't offer alternatives that offer the convenience they are accustomed to. People are still dependent on the system for food, tools, communication, and survival. The solution is replacing the infrastructure and parallel systems.

Start promoting in your campaign:

- Amazon alternatives: Local co-ops, local stores and mom and pop shops, community-run distro networks, eBay, Etsy, secondhand exchanges that funnel some revenue back into the people.
- Meta/Google alternatives: Signal, Matrix, CryptPad, and in-person organizing, print press. Search Engine: Tor, Freenet.org, DuckDuckGo, StartPage, Brave
- Email: ProtonMail, Ledger Mail, Tutanota
- Cloud Storage: Sync.com (end-to-end encrypted), NextCloud (self-hosted, decentralized).
- Big banks: Switch to credit unions, smaller community banking, or decentralized finance platforms
- Corporate media: Zines, underground print, pirate radio, community journalism

Step 5: Measure the Impact

To know it's working, track your wins:

- Number of account deletions or subscription cancellations
- Local contracts lost by the company (school boards, cities, etc.)
- Public backlash or media coverage
- Shareholder action, stock hits, or policy changes
- Expansion of alternative systems (e.g., CSA growth, new distro networks)

Every successful boycott is part of something larger and does not happen overnight. Every boycott is a campaign of attrition, not a flash protest. The goal isn't to make a corporation apologize; it's to erode its credibility, drain its capital base, and replace its function with something people control. Collapse legitimacy first, then replace the infrastructure it once owned, distribution, communication, labor, production, with autonomous, cooperative systems. A real boycott doesn't pause the machine; it rewires the economy beneath it. We're not temporarily targeting a company. We're dismantling the architecture of dependence that sustains it. To end fascism and neoliberal control, we need what corporations already have: structure, logistics, funding, and cultural normalization. We're not entirely reinventing the wheel; we're liberating it from the machine. Reclaiming the tools of organization, logistics, and culture to serve people and Earth before profit. *Here is what the movement needs ASAP*:

Create browser extensions or mobile apps that block or warn users when visiting targeted companies (e.g., "This site is tied to surveillance capitalism — here are 3 alternatives.").

Build auto-switching tools that reroute purchases or searches through ethical platforms: like a boycott-first version of Honey or Rakuten.

Develop a public "corporate criminal database" searchable by brand: that connects everyday products to state violence, labor abuse, or surveillance.

Gamify divestment and Boycotts with leaderboards showing collective wins: cancellations, dollars redirected, contracts broken.

Organize from within. Support whistleblowers, unions, and contractors to destabilize from the inside. Block or slow supply chains through collective action, strikes, and digital sabotage. The machine breaks when its workers stop feeding it. **Narrative Reclaim**: Turn the company's symbols into liabilities. Reframe its slogans, ads, and campaigns into cultural parody and counter-narrative. Make its logo synonymous with destruction, exploitation, or deceit. Once a brand becomes a public embarrassment, it can't maintain political cover.

Remember reputation is everything to the corporate bully, sustained public outcry is the greatest counter weapon.

IV. What Is the Counterworld?

A counterworld is a system built *outside and against* the dominant one. It functions independently of capitalism, state surveillance, and fascist and globalist control. It serves the people and planet, not profit. For anyone whose body, movement, housing, and access to healthcare are constantly monitored, restricted, or priced out of reach, the counterworld is necessity.

Historical examples:

- Spanish anarchist collectives (1936–39): worker-controlled factories, free schools, decentralized food distribution
- Maroon communities: escaped enslaved people forming sovereign zones, producing food, resisting recapture for generations
- Zapatista autonomy zones (1994–present): local governance, food, education, and defense, all outside state control
- Christiania (Denmark, 1971–present): A self-governed anarchist community with its own rules, independent from state control, focusing on collective living, sustainability, and art.

Regenerative Logic: Return to the Living World

The counterworld doesn't mimic capitalism and oligarchic systems with better values. It rejects the logic of domination altogether. The counterworld begins with *you* when you stop supporting the companies that destroy Earth. It is a daily conscious decision. Every dollar, click, and vote for convenience and "normalcy," is a contract with destruction that we all have signed without thinking. It is an unconscious choice we make in some way every day to support, but by implementing simple lifestyle changes and radical acts of self-determination we can cut our corporate dependency and minimize the consistency. Each person must divest from the toxic systems that sustain the two-party duopoly and its machinery of extraction, the systems that exploit people, animals, and the Earth until scarcity and moral collapse are widespread. To build a counterworld is to withdrawal consent from the manufactured consensus that presents itself as the only way, and to reclaim the power to live, create, and relate outside its spell.

- Divest from corporate predators. No longer consume out of convenience.

- Grow your own food, use co-ops, farmers markets= break corporate dependency
- Medicate holistically where safely = exit pharma monopolies and challenge the industrialized health system by eating well and healing the internal root cause.
- Barter + thrift +gift economies = end commodification of everything
- Build shelter and community land projects = refuse to be priced out of survival
- Cultural reclamation = return to ancestral, land-based reciprocal ways of living.

Think and create like a mycelial network, interconnected, underground, resilient. If they cut off one part, the rest grows stronger. This new world requires reconceptualizing everything, from how we live, to how we relate, to how we provide for each other. It's not about piecemeal reforms, it's about total systems reimagination:

- Design life outside rental dependence, medical debt, digital tracking, gig-work exploitation, and corporate food and water control. Decentralize power so no single institution or hierarchy can own the future.
- Build cooperative economies where survival comes before profit, and food, housing, education, and healthcare are treated as collective rights.
- Teach for critical thought and ecological awareness instead of from obedience and the status quo.

The counterworld grows every time someone chooses to step out of the digital script and into real autonomy. A lot of it starts online in group chats, Discord servers, mutual aid pages, burner accounts, but it only becomes real when it moves off-screen into boycotts, direct action, food co-ops, community gardens, shared housing, strike funds, and local economies that don't run on extraction. When one crew figures out how to feed themselves, share resources, or step back from exploitative jobs, it becomes a live example other people can copy and remix. The counterworld isn't a perfect alt-universe or some future utopia, it's a constant process of trying things, failing, adjusting, and learning how not to dominate each other. Sovereignty here isn't about dipping out and pretending you don't need anyone. It's self-governance in service of collective freedom. We get out together or we don't. Stay in solidarity with the people still stuck in the systems we're trying to change. And along the way: know your rights, think for yourself, question everything, don't bypass the hard stuff, build community, divest, disrupt, and redirect.

Essential Syllabus for Movement Builders: On Tyranny — *Timothy Snyder* · **Ur-Fascism** — *Umberto Eco* **American Fascists** — *Chris Hedges* · **Emergent Strategy** — *Adrienne Maree Brown* **Manufacturing Consent** — *Noam Chomsky & Edward Herman* · **Propaganda** — *Edward Bernays* · **The Civic Foundations of Fascism** — *Dylan Riley* · **The Wretched of the Earth** —Frantz Fanon · **Sacred Economics** — *Charles Eisenstein* · **Critical Path** — *Buckminster Fuller* · **Biomimicry** — *Janine Benyus* · **This Is an Uprising** — *Mark & Paul Engler* · **The Ecology of Freedom** — *Murray Bookchin* · **Pedagogy of the Oppressed** — *Paulo Freire* · **Meditations** — *Marcus Aurelius* ·**Civil Disobedience** — *Henry David Thoreau* · **Nonviolent Communication** — *Marshall B. Rosenberg*

www.ingramcontent.com/pod-product-compliance
Lightning Source LLC
Chambersburg PA
CBHW052131030426
42337CB00028B/5113